YOUR KNOWLEDGE HAS VALUE

- We will publish your bachelor's and master's thesis, essays and papers

- Your own eBook and book - sold worldwide in all relevant shops

- Earn money with each sale

Upload your text at www.GRIN.com and publish for free

Bibliographic information published by the German National Library:

The German National Library lists this publication in the National Bibliography; detailed bibliographic data are available on the Internet at http://dnb.dnb.de .

Imprint:

Copyright © 2014 GRIN Verlag
Print and binding: Books on Demand GmbH, Norderstedt Germany
ISBN: 9783668939554

This book at GRIN:

https://www.grin.com/document/462250

Somdip Dey

Efficient Data Input/Output (I/O) for Finite Difference Time Domain (FDTD). Computation on Graphics Processing Unit (GPU)

GRIN Verlag

GRIN - Your knowledge has value

Since its foundation in 1998, GRIN has specialized in publishing academic texts by students, college teachers and other academics as e-book and printed book. The website www.grin.com is an ideal platform for presenting term papers, final papers, scientific essays, dissertations and specialist books.

Visit us on the internet:

http://www.grin.com/

http://www.facebook.com/grincom

http://www.twitter.com/grin_com

EFFICIENT DATA INPUT/OUTPUT (I/O) FOR FINITE DIFFERENCE TIME DOMAIN (FDTD) COMPUTATION ON GRAPHICS PROCESSING UNIT (GPU)

A DISSERTATION SUBMITTED TO THE UNIVERSITY OF MANCHESTER
FOR THE DEGREE OF MASTER OF SCIENCE
IN THE FACULTY OF ENGINEERING AND PHYSICAL SCIENCES

2014

By
Somdip Dey
School of Computer Science

Contents

Word Count: 14,100

List of Tables

List of Figures

Abstract

Due to recent advancement in technology, one of the popular ways of achieving performance with respect to execution time of programs is by utilizing massive parallelism power of GPU-based accelerator computing along with CPU computing. In GPU-based accelerator computing, the data intensive or computationally intensive part is computed on the GPU whereas the simple yet complex instructions are computed on the CPU in order to achieve massive speedup in execution time of the computer program executed on the computer system.

In physics, especially in electromagnetism, Finite-Difference Time-Domain (FDTD) is a popular numerical analysis method, which is used to solve the set of Maxwells partial differential equations to unify and relate electric field with magnetic field. Since FDTD method is computationally intensive and has high level of parallelism in the computational implementation, for this reason for past few years researchers are trying to compute the computationally intensive part of FDTD methods on the GPU instead of CPU. Although computing parallelized parts of FDTD algorithms on the GPU achieve very good performance, but fail to gain very good speedup in execution time because of the very high latency between the CPU and GPU. Calculation results at each FDTD time-step is supposed to be produced and saved on the hard disk of the system. This can be called as data output of the FDTD methods, and the overlapping of data output and computation of the field values at next time step can not be performed simultaneously. Because of this and latency gap between the CPU and GPU, there is a bottleneck in the performance of the data output of the GPU. This problem can be regarded as the inefficient performance of data input/output (I/O) of FDTD methods on GPU.

Hence, this project focuses on this aforementioned problem and addresses to find solutions to improve the efficiency of the data I/O of FDTD computation on GPGPU (General Purpose Graphics Processing Unit).

Keywords: data I/O; buffer; Finite difference methods; FDTD; time domain analysis; hardware; acceleration; high performance computing; parallel programming; parallel architectures; GPU; graphics processing unit; parallel computing; CUDA; OpenACC; multi-core computing

Acknowledgements

I would like to thank my Supervisor, Fumie Costen, for her endless support and patience in answering every question that I had while prusuing the project and preparing the thesis. Without her presence this thesis could not have been written properly.

I also want to mention my family, who have always supported me, especifically my parents, Soma Dey and Sudip Dey, for giving me the blessings and boosts that drove me to success in life.

Finaly, I would also like to thank Buraq Abdul Qader for providing valuable insights and technical knowledge that made it easier for me to pursue this project. A special thanks to Tanaya Gopal, Rashmi vivek Joshi, Madhuri Raju and Harshini M. Kumar for putting up to my nuisance and mischieves, and for being there to support me at times when needed.

Chapter 1

Introduction

1.1 Computation in Electromagnetism

In the world of physics, there are four fundamental forces in nature: strong force, weak force, gravitational force and electromagentic force. Electromagnetism is the field of study to review and relate different electro-magnetic fields and study the interactions between electrically charged particles and uncharged magnetic force fields with electrical conductors. But as the world advanced towards the age of Digital Technology, the techniques and methods related to electromagnetism also grew in complexity. It was no longer possible to calculate the complex formulas, which are associated to electromagnetism, just by hand and paper. This demanded for calculating these complex techniques in computers by means of computer programs. Even though computers can execute and compute these methods very efficiently and as quickly as possible but some of the technique requires much more computational resources and time of execution.

1.1.1 Maxwell's Equations

In the middle of 19th century, eminent mathematical physicist James C. Maxwell related the electric and magnetic field compnents and studied how these fields alter each other by means of charges and current. He proposed a set of partial differential equations, which linked all electric and magnetic field components, and these set of partial differential equations are known as the Maxwell's Equations. Maxwell's Equations along with Lorentz force [1] law form the foundations of electromagnetism and classical electrodynamics. The Maxwells Equations unify and unite Faradays Law, Amperes Law, Gauss Law for the electric field and for the magnetic field, Ohms Law, etc.

Over the years many numerical analysis methods were proposed and implemented to solve the Maxwell's equations efficienctly and accurately, and one such popular method is the Finite-Difference Time-Domain.

1.1.2   Finite-Difference Time-Domain (FDTD)

Finite-Difference Time-Domain(FDTD) aids to to discretise the Maxwell's partial differential equations by using Yee's algorithm [3], which was proposed by Kan Yee, to solve both the electric and magentic fields in time and space.

The abstraction performed by FDTD method to solve Maxwell's equations, makes it easy to compute and calculate the set of partial differential equations on a computer. FDTD method consist of update equations, which updates the value of electric and magnetic fieds based on the latest available values of magnetic fields and electric fields respectively. For example, to calculate H (magnetic field) at $(t + 0.5\Delta t)$ time-step, the value of E (electric field) at t time-step is required. In brief, the way in which FDTD is calculated is: Calculate H from recently available E value, calculate D (electric flux) from the recently available H value, calculate E from the recently available D value. Because of the way by which FDTD method is calculated, there are high level of parallelization in the computation of the method.

Maxwell's Equations and FDTD method is mentioned comprehensively in chapter 2, which aids the motive and objective of this thesis.

1.2   Computational Parallelization Techniques & GPGPU

"For over a decade prophets have voiced the contention that the organization of a single computer has reached its limits and that truly signif-
icant advances can be made only by interconnection of a multiplicity
of computers in such a manner as to permit cooperative solution."
- Gene M. Amdahl, (1967) [4]

Amdahls Law, which is the de facto of the parallel and multicore computing world,

---

[1]In electromagnetism, the Lorentz force combines the electric and magnetic forces on a point charge due to electromagnetic fields

states that even if an algorithm is parallelized, it starts from serial execution and then again ends serially although major part of the algorithm is parallelized. Thus even though an algorithm is parallelized, but its performance with respect to execution is dependent on both serialized and parallelized part. For FDTD method, major part of the calculations involed, are parallelizable in nature, and hence is subject to very good performance with respect to time of execution if the parallel execution part is correctly implemented.

Now, performance of a parallelized task depends on various factors but the major factors that really affect the performance are good parallelized hardware support and good parallelized algortihm & programming techniques.

1.2.1   Parallel Computer Architecture

According to study materials publsihed by J. R. Gurd [5], a basic computer architeture consists of the CPU (Central Processing Unit) and the memory. Here, the memory consists of two parts, the fixed *Code* and the changeable *Data*, which define the program being executed. When execution of the program starts on a computer, the *Code* part of the memory holds the fixed portion of the program, which will not change during the execution, such as formula required for calculation, etc., and the initial data of the program, which defines the computation such as the input data, the initial values of required variables, etc., are being held in the *Data* part of the memory. The CPU consists of a Program Counter (PC), which starts by pointing to the first instrutction to be executed. As the program progresses in execution, the current instruction is fetched from the Code memory and the PC is incremented to point to the current execution instruction. All the CPU states such as registers, conditional codes, etc. except the PC, are part of the Data memory. The CPU follows Instrutction Execution Cycle at Program level, which means how many instructions being executed during one clock cycle. Exectuion of a program may consists of the following steps:

- Reading data from the *Data* memory Considered as 'Read access'

- Perform the required operations

- Write the result back to the *Data* memory Considered as 'Write Access'

- Increment the program counter or assign a new value to the PC

During the execution, all the steps mentioned abve or few of them may be performed depending on the program. This is commonly known as 'von Neumann Computational Model' [6, 7], which consists of sequential computation.

With a careful analysis it can be found that when a program is executed , the processor / CPU[2] spends most of the time in moving the data from and to the memory than calculating. For example, if a processor has to perform the following tasks:

```
1       a=6
2       b=12
3       c=a+b
```

And, if the time taken to execute these tasks together is assumed to be T secs then, the processor first have to fecth the value '6' from the memory and assign it to 'a', then do the same fecthing and assigning operations to variable 'b'. After that calculate 'a+b' and then assign the resulted value to 'c'. It should be kept in mind that 'a', 'b' and 'c' are also variables that are on the memory. Now if it is considered that the time taken to fetch the values and copy back the values to the memory be t_1 secs, and the time taken to perform the matehmatical operation of 'a+b', i.e. adding the values, be t_2 secs, such that the total time taken by the operations performed is $t_1 + t_2 = T$. Then, $t_2 << T$, implying that t_2 is very very less than T and most of the time of execution is spent in dealing with memory realted operations rather than mathematical operations. Therefore, it can be said that performance of a program with respect to execution time, is actually dependent on the performance of the memory in the computer system.

This problem of performance delay is incurred due to the memory latency gap. Before executing any operation, it first has to be fetched from the main memory and then executed in the CPU. And because of the gap between the memory and the CPU [8, 9] the time of execution is increased. Please refer to Fig. 1.1 for a basic block diagram of CPU and memory, and the memory interface to connect these two. It should also be kept in mind that although the gap between the memory and CPU increases the time of execution, but this can be hardly noticed because the total time taken for execution may be in seconds. But when compared to the time to perform mathematical operations or operations, which do not include memory access, the time taken by operations to perform some kind of memory access is huge. In 1996, Hennessy and Patterson [7]

---

[2]In sequential computing a processor and a CPU is condisered to be the same thing. But with the advancement of technology and with the incorporation of many CPUs in one system i.e. multi-core, the terms CPU and processor may have differed. Some processor manufacturers now call each core as CPU and the chip containing these cores as processor. But for this example, the CPU and the processor should be considered the same.

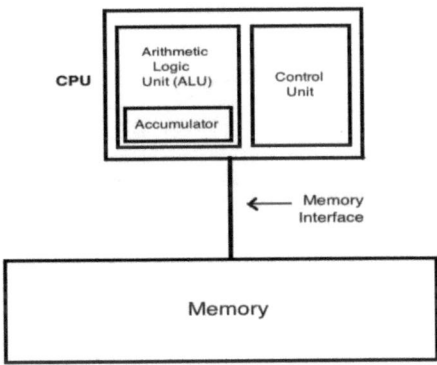

Figure 1.1: Block Diagram of CPU and Memory Architecture

introduced the concept of Cycles Per Instruction (CPI), which is the the average number of clock cycles required to execute one instruction. Now, if it is assumed that to perform a mathematical operation such as addition i.e. '+', is 1 CPI, then to perform a fecth data from the memory operation can take around 10 CPI, which in comparison is very high. This gives a fair idea regarding how the execution time is affected by the memory latency gap.

To deal with this probelm, many techniques have been introduced as technology advanced. One of the best known methods is to accomodate faster memory on the chip of the CPU, which are called cache memories[3]. Since, cache memory is not the focus of this thesis, therefore a detailed performance gain using caches is not discussed in this thesis.

In modern computing era (post 1960), due to increase in complex workloads and parallelizable tasks, there has been a rise in parallel and multi-core computing. Now a days computer systems hardly consist of single core CPU. Since gaining performance with respect to time of execution, is of upmost important now, so the main focus is on parallel computing (parallel computers or parallel algorithmic techniques).

Parallel computer systems [5] may have many different architecture but all these architectures can be generalized into following:

- Shared Memory Multiprocessor Architecture

---

[3]Cache is a smaller, faster memory used by CPU to reduce the average time of accessing data from the main memory.

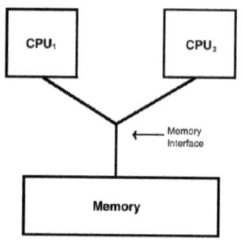

Figure 1.2: Diagramatic Represntation of Shared Memory Parallel Computer Architecture consisting of two CPUs

- Distributed Memory Multicomputer (Distributed Memory Parallel Computer Architecture)

Again, in general the shared memory multiprocessor can be of two type:

- Shared Memory Parallel Computer Architecture

- Split Shared Memory Parallel Computer Architecture

Shared Memory Parallel Computer Architecture: In this architecture, the system consists of more than one CPU but the memory interface is the same as the sequential computer architecture. Write access to the memory is same as the sequntial architecture but the read access to memory is different. The read access requests are tagged with the identity of the issuing CPU so that the data can be returned to the correct CPU. Refer to Fig.1.2.

Split Shared Memory Parallel Computer Architecture: In this architecture, the memory is split into many memory banks, which are accessed by many CPUs in the system. But the CPUs are connected to the memory banks by 'interconnect'. The interconnect directs each memory access from CPUs to the appropriate memory bank and memory addresses are allocated across the memory banks in different ways such as interleaved, in blocks, etc., as long as there is no clash or contention of memory access from different CPUs. The interconnect can be implemented hardware wise in different ways, but the most popular method is by implementing as a bus, which is cheap to

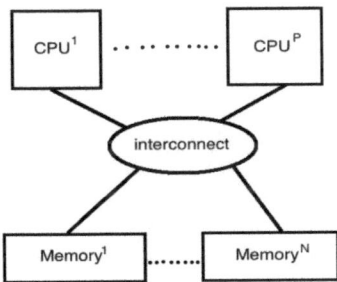

Figure 1.3: Diagramatic Represntation of Split Shared Memory Parallel Computer Architecture consisting of 'P' number of CPUs connected to the Memory, which has 'N' number of Memory Banks, via Interconnect

implement. The bus interconnect has its own limitations such as limited number of CPUs and memory banks can be connected using this. Refer to Fig.1.3.

Distributed Memory Parallel Computer Architecture: In this architecture, the memory is distributed physically amongst 'P' number of CPUs. Thus this architecture with each 'CPU with memory' resembles the von Neumann, i.e. sequential, computer architecture, and the system is called a Distributed Memory Multicomputer[4]. Refer to Fig.1.4. This architecture is actually influenced by the following:

- By co-locating a CPU and a memory bank and by making them share the same bus interface, increases the capacity of the bus.

- During the exectuion of a program, many of the required variables are private to each thread[5]. Therefore, by placing the private variables in the co-located memory reduces the use of bus interconnect.

There are many variants of Distributed Memory Parallel Computer Architecture such as Distributed Shared Memory (DSM), where the available addresses are shared across

---

[4]Here the term computer in the word 'multicomputer', is referred to CPU with some memory attached to it.

[5]A thread is the smallest sequence of a program, which can be managed independently by a scheduler of an Operating System and run in a shared memory space. Whereas, a process has its own memory space and when many processes are executed together, they run in separate memory spaces.

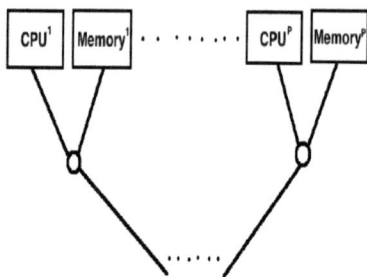

Figure 1.4: Diagramatic Represntation of Distributed Memory Parallel Computer Architecture

the memory banks with single address space, or Distributed Memory (DM) with multiple address spaces accross the system, where each CPU is only allowed to issue addresses to its own local memory bank, etc. Another popular trend is cluster computing, where the memory is shared at computer level in sub-parts to make a parallel structure. Since these hardware techniques are not within the scope of this thesis, hence not discussed in details.

In the next section, the different ways of parallelising algorithms and implement them as programming techniques, are provided.

1.2.2   Parallel Algorithms & Programs

In the study materials provide by J. Gurd [5], it was noted that although different programs/applications in the world of High Performance Computing (HPC) have different structures but they still have some common characterisitics such as:

- Use of discrete approximation for calculation prupose

- A foundation of mathematical model underneath the application for the caclculation

- An algorithm to 'animate' the underpinning mathematical model so that it can be used for digital computation

Parallel Algorithms: With a closer analysis on the parallel applications it can be noticed that there are some evident patterns in which the program is parallelised, which can be classified as the following:

- **Data parallelism:** In this type, there is an existence of some large data domain, where similar kind of computation is to be done on the data of that domain. Sometimes the data can be computed paralelly very easily and hence those are called embarassingly parallel.

- **Reduction parallelism:** In this type, there is an existence of some large data domain, where it is necessary to compute some kind of global function which is common to the entire domain. This type of parallelism is not always obvious like data parallelism, but it would depend on the problem, which is being computed.

- **Divideandconquer parallelism:** This type of parallelism is more of an algorithmic approach than it is a pattern. Many sequential tasks can be visualized as an aggregate of many smaller parallelisable tasks. In order to solve the problem as a whole, the whole task is divided into small tasks and then computed parallely. But to approach a problem like this, it is the programmers responsibility to algorithmicly approach the parallilising technique.

- **Task parallelism:** Here, the task consists of multiple distinct computations, each of which can be computed simultaneously. In this way, different procedures can be applied to parts of data domain to create parallel tasks and hence each computation may take different execution time.

The aforementioned parallelising algorithmic technqiues can be implemented as a computer program in the three most popular ways:

- **Data Sharing (Thread-Based):** When a process consists of smaller light-weight tasks, commonly known as Threads (as mentioned earlier in previous sub-section1.2.1), and these threads are executed on the same memory by using seperate blocks / priorities for each thread, then this parallel programming style can be called Thread-Based Data Sharing. One of the most popular application programming interface (API) in academia and industry, which supports shared memory parallel programming is **OpenMP** [10]. OpenMP API deals to manage the threads implicitly. There are few other libraries and APIs that support this methodology but are not as popular as OpenMP. OpenMP is multi-platform and supports programming languages such as C, C++ and Fortran.

- **Message Passing (Process Based):** When a large problem consists of several processes, it is possible to execute more than one process at the same time. This is achieved by co-operating the execution of different processes and by executing these processes on seperate processors with seperate memory. The processors co-ordinate the execution by passing messages and hence the name is derived from there. One of the most popular message passing programming techniques devised is **Message Passing Interface (MPI)** [11]. MPI library supports major programming languages such as C, C++, Fortran and Java.

- **Hybrid Programming Technique:** In hybrid programming scheme, both the techniques mentioned above can be implemented together in order to achieve even better performance. Although the performance will completely depend on the problem itself and the way the problem is parallelised to gain better performance. One example of this technique can be to use MPI to compute seperate processes parallely, whereas using OpenMP at the same time inside MPI to parallelise each process into multiple threads and compute them simultaneously.

It should be kept in mind that there are many other variants and features related to the aforementioned programming techniques but those are not within the scope of this thesis and hence not pursued anymore to be worth mentioning here.

Now, although a High Performance System can consist of mixture of the parallel hardware architecture and parallel programming techniques, which are mentioned above (sub-sections 1.2.1, 1.2.2), but the performance of the system can not be evaluated till there are some firm methods to compare its performance with some other standardised methods.

Measuring Performance: Performance of a program in HPC world is evaluated by two ways, either by assessing floating point operations performed per second ($flop/s$) or by assessing the execution time. The term ($flop/s$) is mostly used to evaluate performance of parallel architecture hardware, which is done by measuring how many floating point calculations are performed in a second. Another method of measuring performance is by meauring the time of execution of the program using P processors and then comparing it with the time of execution for 1 processor. The main concern is to assess the performance and success of a parallel program by evaluating the performance on a variety of different parallel configurations.

1.2.3 Emerging Parallelization Techniques: GPGPU

The hardware and algorithmic techniques, which are already available for parallelising complex tasks, are more than sufficient to compute most algorithms efficiently, but due to the advancement of technology and never ending thirst of developing more advanced technology, have led the way of parallelization into different routes.

Post 1980, the world of technology saw the development of a new technolgy, which changed the way people used to visualise computer graphics. That innovative technology was the Graphics Processing Unit (GPU), which used to accelerate the graphics processing in order to enhance visual representation on a computer. In a GPU [12–14] the graphics are processed by multiple shader cores, which are the basic basic processing unit of a GPU. These shader cores are used to shade an image (pixels) or to provide effects to an image by the means of a computer programming technique called 'shaders' [12]. Shader calculates rendering [6] effects on the graphics hardware and produces the image as an output. A basic GPU architecture consists of multiple shader cores, which are capable of shading multiple pixel on an image. GPU had the inherent property of parallel computing from the beginning and this ideology of computing multiple pixels uising shader cores, gave rise to the idea of General Purpose Graphics Processing Unit for computing multiple calculations at the same time. The notion, General Purpose Graphics Processing Unit (GPGPU) means to be able to compute general calculations on GPU, instead of using the GPU just for graphical processing purpose.

Modern GPUs [15–17] have many processing cores, which are called streaming multiprocessors (SMs) and each processor may has one or multiple stream processors (SPs) (refer to Fig.1.5). When a parallelisable work is computed on GPGPUs, the CPU computes the serial parts of the program/applicationbeing executed and the parallelsied (repetitive tasks) parts are computed on the GPU (refer to Fig.1.6). For this thesis, GPGPU of Nvidia are used. CUDA [1,2,15,18,19] is a parallel computing platform and programming model invented by NVIDIA, which enables the programmer and users to significantly increase the computing performance by harnessing the parallelization power of GPUs. More details regarding parallel computing on GPGPU are provided in Chapter 3.

As a part of the research conducted for the purpose of this thesis, a survey (refer to appendix A) was pursued to evaluate the performance, ease of use and futurescope of

---

[6]Rendering is the process of generating an image from a model

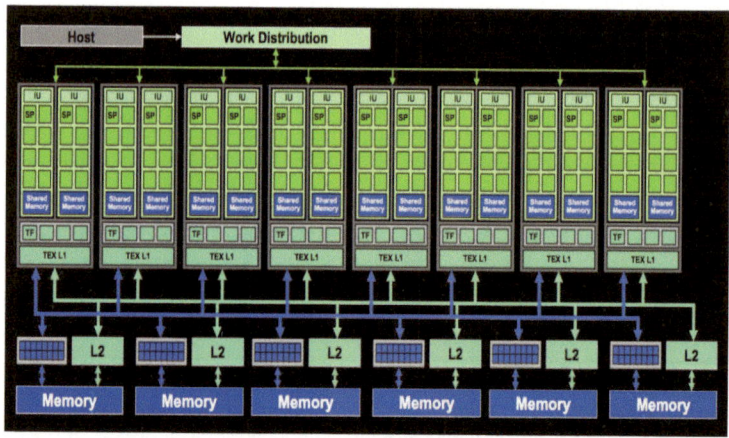

Figure 1.5: Nvidia GPUs Fundamental Architecture with 16 Streaming Multiprocessor, each with 8 stream processors (SPs) (128 stream processors in total) and 8 parallel texture mapping units (TMUs), which are used to address and filter the textures of images on the graphics hardware

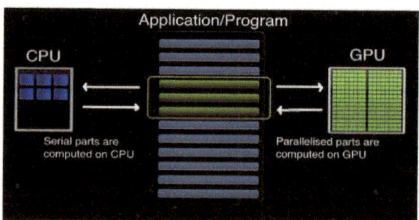

Figure 1.6: Parallel Execution on GPGPU

CUDA programming (GPGPU Computing) along with other popular parallel programming techniques such as OpenMP and MPI. The survey was distributed in the form of email and over ResearchGate website, which is a social networking site for scientists and researchers to share their research findings and ideas. The survey was completed by 39 participants, who are professionals from the industry and the academia related to High Performance Computing. The typical questions in the survey were to evaluate the performance gained, ease of imeplementation and future scope of wide usability of either of OpenMP, MPI and CUDA parallel computing techniques. The outcome of the survey was:

OpenMP

- Ease of Use/Implementation: 72% agreed strongly

- Performance Gained: 14% agreed strongly

- Has potential to be used more in future: 9% agreed strongly

MPI

- Ease of Use/Implementation: 23% agreed strongly

- Performance Gained: 73% agreed strongly

- Has potential to be used more in future: 0% agreed strongly

CUDA Programming

- Ease of Use/Implementation: 73% agreed strongly

- Performance Gained: 91% agreed strongly

- Has potential to be used more in future: 91% agreed strongly (see Fig. 1.7)

[In the above survey result, the perecentage (%) respresents the perecentage of the survey respondents/participants. It should also be kept in mind that the performance gained by MPI technique is eqaully comparable with the performance gained in CUDA GPGPU technique, but future scope of CUDA is much more evident than MPI's according to the survey. The survey was completely based on the study of the ease of implementation and performance gained based on that implementation.]

Although for this survey, the participants' pool is very small to determine the actual trend in the industry but still this gives the hint of where the trend is leading to.

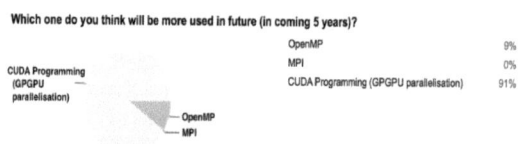

Figure 1.7: Result of survey question on 'Which one has more potential to be used in future?'

CUDA programming for GPGPU is easy to implement by programmers and the implemntation yields very good performance, and may be because of these reasons more people will prefer CUDA as parallel computing programming technique in near future. As a conlcusion this survey re-assures that the topic pursued as part of this thesis is of high importance and will definitely help programmers using CUDA programming technique.

Since, GPGPU computing as part of high performance computing is relatively new in the industry, it has both its advantages and limitations.

1.3 The Problem and The Objective

GPGPU computing is also called Accelerator based computing, i.e. a GPGPU is called an accelerator, which accelerates the computation. When a computation is performed using GPGPU, the CPU is regarded as the 'host' and the GPU is considered as the 'device'. In typical high performance computing world, the bootleneck in performance is mainly created because of the latency gap between the memory and the CPU as discussed in sub-section 1.2.1 and the same thing is true for GPGPU computing.

GPU is connected to the chipset[7] of the computer system via PCI Express bus, which is also known as Peripheral Component Interconnect Express (PCI-e). The GPU, CPU and the main memory (RAM) all interacts using this PCI-e bus and becuase of the latency gap between these three, there is a bottleneck in the overall performance gain.

When a parallelized program is computed on the GPGPU, first the data is copied from the memory to the GPU and after computation the data is written back to the

---

[7]Chipset is a set of electronic components in the integrated circuit of the motherboard, which manages communiction between the CPU, memory and other peripehral devices

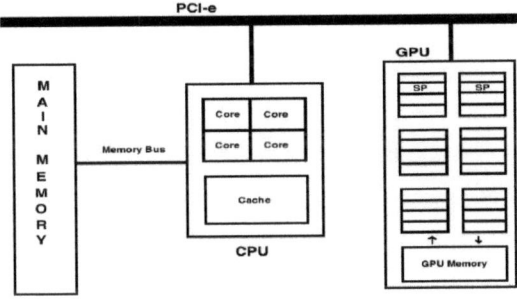

Figure 1.8: Communication between Memory-CPU-GPU via PCI-e Bus

memory from the GPU using the PCI-e bus (Refer to Fig. 1.8). Thus for every computation, data has to be copied to and fro device-host-memory[8]. Although the computation is very fast in GPGPU, but because of the gap between the device-host-memory
due to the communication via PCI-e, the bottleneck in the performance is generated. So
far no effective method has been invented to deal with this problem. Again, CUDA programming for GPGPU computing requires the programmer to manage the data copied
to and fro memory on the GPU for computation purpose by invoking some CUDA
functions such as $cudaMemcpy()$. This made it even difficult for programmers to
write a program in CUDA. But to solve this problem, Nvidia introduced a new programming model in CUDA 6.0 programming language, named Unified Memory [20].
In Unified CUDA memory technique, the whole memory is viewed as a single unified
block of memory (see Fig. 1.9), but this technique still does not improve the aforementioned problem of memory latency gap. Unified memory concept was introduced to
reduce the effort of development, but to gain good performance, the programmer still
needs to manage the data copied to and fro.

In FDTD method, to calculate and update H, E and D values, data have to be
copied and written back to and fro the memory to the GPU (device). Although performance of computation of FDTD algorithm on GPGPU is very good but still because
of the bootleneck generated due to the latency gap between the GPU and the memory,
hinders the true performance that might has been achieved using GPGPU computing
without this problem.

---

[8]Device is the GPU, Host is the CPU

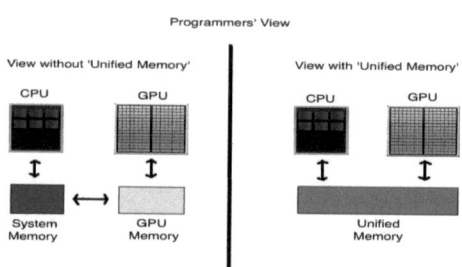

Figure 1.9: View of 'Unified Memory' Concept of CUDA 6.0 Programming Language

The Objective: Therefore the main objective of this thesis is to develop, implement and evaluate a method/technique to reduce the bootleneck created because of the latency gap between the device-host-memory in order to achieve highest performance and efficiency from GPGPU computation for data input/output (I/O) of FDTD method. Another objective is that this proposed method should work properly when accomodated into FDTD algorithm, even for random data points on the grid for data I/O of FDTD method.

In this thesis, a novel apporach to this problem is proposed and the evaluation results of the proposed techniques are also discussed later in Chapters (4, 5) in order to evaluate and validate the effectiveness of the proposed technique.

While preparing this thesis, there was no one academic manuscript, which compiles all the fundamental logics of FDTD method, its computation on GPGPU and increasing the efficiency of data input/output of FDTD computation on GPGPU. Therefore, this thesis deals to cover the following areas:

- Provide the fundamental logic behind Finite-Difference Time-Domain (FDTD) method

- Provide basic understanding of computing FDTD method on CPU and on GPGPU

- Provide solution to the throughput problem, i.e. the latency gap between Memory-CPU-GPU, in order to increase the efficiency of data input/output (I/O) of FDTD method

1.4 Thesis Overview

In the Introduction (Chapter 1), few of the basic concepts of parallel computing, which are essential for this thesis, are mentioned along with a brief review of the problem, which is being dealt for the purpose of this research project. In Chapter 2 the important equations, which are related to FDTD method, are discussed along with the implmentation guidlines of FDTD algorithm in a computer. Chapter 3 explores the methods of computing FDTD algorithm on GPGPU using CUDA programming. Chapter 4 discusses the solution proposed to solve the latency gap between the memory and the device (GPU) and generate more efficiency of data input/output (I/O) for FDTD computation on GPGPU. In chapter 5, the proposed method is evaluated for performance and validated for accuracy, and the results are discussed. In the end, in Chapter 6 the conclusion for the overall thesis is provided along with future scope of the proposed methodology.

1.5 Original Contribution

This thesis presents the authors original contribution in the following areas:

- Survey to evaluate the future-scope of CUDA technology and GPGPU computing in the parallel computing and high performance computing world

- Development and implementation of the solution to increase the efficiency of data input/output (I/O) of FDTD computation on GPGPU (Main Objective)

- Evalutation and validation of the implemented solution

Table 1.1: Major Abbreviations Used In Chapter 1

API	- Application Programming Interface
CPI	- Cycles Per Instruction
CPU	- Central Processing Unit
DM	- Distributed Memory
DSM	- Distributed Shared Memory
FDTD	- Finite-Difference Time-Domain
$flop/s$	- Floating Point Operations per Second
GPU	- General Purpose Graphics Processing Unit
GPGPU	- Graphics Processing Unit
HPC	- High Performance Computing
MPI	- Message Passing Interface
PC	- Program Counter
PCI-e	- Peripheral Component Interconnect Express
RAM	- Random Access Memory
SM	- Streaming Multiprocessors
SP	- Streaming Processors
TMU	- Texture Mapping Units

Chapter 2

Electromagnetism & Finite-Difference Time-Domain - Overview

In this chapter some of the relevant and related overviews on Electromagnetism and Finite-Difference Time-Domain, are provided so that it is easier to understand the implemented methodology, which is mentioned in this dissertation.

Electromagnetism is the field of study in physics that relates time-varying electric and magnetic fields together into unified quantities. Till the middle of 19th century, scientists have believed electric and magnetic fields to be independent of each other. But after extensive research in these fields of studies new results have proved otherwise. It was Ampere's and Faraday's laws, which were the first to relate the motion of both the physical quantities. Then after unifying the contemporary knowledge on electric and magnetic fields, James Clerk Maxwell proposed a set of 20 differential equations that related all electric and magnetic components together. These equations are widely known as Maxwell's Equations, which are a set of partial differential equations that together with Lorentz Force law, form the basis of electromagnetism and few other fields of studies in physics such as classical optics and electric circuits.

2.1 Maxwell's Equations

James Clerk Maxwell published primitive form of the set of partial differential equations during the middle of 19th Century, which tries to unite and relate different variable fields in electromagnetism such as electric field, magnetic field, electric flux density, magnetic flux density, conduction current density and charge density. A paper published by Costen (2005), which studied the computational modeling of applications of Ultra Wide Bandwidth (UWB) signals [21] and hence studied different methods of FDTD to solve Maxwell?s Equations. According to this paper, in MKS units, Electric field E (Volt/Meter), magnetic field H (Ampere/Meter), electric flux density D (Coulomb/[Meter]^2), magnetic flux density B (Tesla) , conduction current density J (Ampere/[Meter]^2), and charge density ρ (Coulomb/[Meter]^3), satisfy Faraday's law, Ampere's Law, Gauss' Law for the electric field and for the magnetic field, Ohm's Law. The relevant equations that are associated with these laws are as follows: Faraday's law,

$$\nabla \times E = -\frac{\partial B}{\partial t}, \tag{2.1}$$

Ampere's law,

$$\nabla \times H = J + \frac{\partial D}{\partial t}, \tag{2.2}$$

Gauss's law for the electric field,

$$\nabla \bullet D = \rho, \tag{2.3}$$

Gauss's law for the magnetic field,

$$\nabla \bullet B = 0, \tag{2.4}$$

The Ohm's law,

$$J = \sigma E, \tag{2.5}$$

where σ is a conductivity, which is a material dependent parameter and ρ is electric charge density.

If free space is considered then according to Yee's (1966) studies [3]:

$$D = \epsilon E \tag{2.6}$$

$$B = \mu H \tag{2.7}$$

$$J = 0 \tag{2.8}$$

where $\epsilon_0 = \epsilon$ (Farad/Meter) is the free space permittivity and $\mu_0 = \mu$ (Henry/Meter) is the permeability of free space. (More regarding Yee's studies will be discussed in next section ??) And therefore, the equations Eq.(2.1) and Eq.(2.7) are re-written in vector format:

$$\nabla \times \boldsymbol{E} = (\frac{\partial E_z}{\partial y} - \frac{\partial E_y}{\partial z})\mathbf{i}_x + (\frac{\partial E_x}{\partial z} - \frac{\partial E_z}{\partial x})\mathbf{i}_y + (\frac{\partial E_y}{\partial x} - \frac{\partial E_x}{\partial y})\mathbf{i}_z = \quad (2.9)$$

$$-\frac{\partial \boldsymbol{B}}{\partial t} = -\mu\frac{\partial(H_x + H_y + H_z)}{\partial t}.$$

And the equation Eq.(2.2) is re-written in vector format using Eq.(2.6) and Eq.(2.8) as:

$$\nabla \times \boldsymbol{H} = (\frac{\partial H_z}{\partial y} - \frac{\partial H_y}{\partial z})\mathbf{i}_x + (\frac{\partial H_x}{\partial z} - \frac{\partial H_z}{\partial x})\mathbf{i}_y + (\frac{\partial H_y}{\partial x} - \frac{\partial H_x}{\partial y})\mathbf{i}_z \quad (2.10)$$

$$= \epsilon\frac{\partial(E_x + E_y + E_z)}{\partial t}$$

where $\mathbf{i}_x$, $\mathbf{i}_y$ and $\mathbf{i}_z$ are the unit vectors in x, y and z directions. Therefore, Eq.(2.9) can now be expressed in a scalar manner as follows:

$$\frac{\partial E_z}{\partial y} - \frac{\partial E_y}{\partial z} = -\mu\frac{\partial H_x}{\partial t} \qquad (2.11)$$

$$\frac{\partial E_x}{\partial z} - \frac{\partial E_z}{\partial x} = -\mu\frac{\partial H_y}{\partial t} \qquad (2.12)$$

$$\frac{\partial E_y}{\partial x} - \frac{\partial E_x}{\partial y} = -\mu\frac{\partial H_z}{\partial t}. \qquad (2.13)$$

And Eq.(2.10) can be expressed in a scalar manner as follows:

$$\frac{\partial H_z}{\partial y} - \frac{\partial H_y}{\partial z} = \epsilon\frac{\partial E_x}{\partial t} \qquad (2.14)$$

$$\frac{\partial H_x}{\partial z} - \frac{\partial H_z}{\partial x} = \epsilon\frac{\partial E_y}{\partial t} \qquad (2.15)$$

$$\frac{\partial H_y}{\partial x} - \frac{\partial H_x}{\partial y} = \epsilon\frac{\partial E_z}{\partial t} \qquad (2.16)$$

For conductive materials, equations Eq.(2.2), Eq.(2.5) and Eq.(2.6) produce:

$$\nabla \times \boldsymbol{H} = \sigma \boldsymbol{E} + \frac{\partial \boldsymbol{D}}{\partial t} = \sigma \boldsymbol{E} + \frac{\partial \epsilon \boldsymbol{E}}{\partial t} = \left(\sigma + \epsilon \frac{\partial}{\partial t}\right) \boldsymbol{E} \quad (2.17)$$

$$= \left(\sigma + \epsilon \frac{\partial}{\partial t}\right) \boldsymbol{E} = (\sigma + \jmath \omega \epsilon_0 \epsilon_r) \boldsymbol{E} = \jmath \omega \epsilon_0 \left(\epsilon_r + \frac{\sigma}{\jmath \omega \epsilon_0}\right) \boldsymbol{E} = \frac{\partial \epsilon \boldsymbol{E}}{\partial t} = \frac{\partial \boldsymbol{D}}{\partial t}$$

where,

$$\epsilon = \epsilon_r \epsilon_0 - \jmath \frac{\sigma}{\omega} = \epsilon_0 \left(\epsilon_r - \jmath \frac{\sigma}{\omega \epsilon_0}\right). \quad (2.18)$$

and the frequency of the wave $= (\frac{\omega}{2\pi})$, which is propagating the medium. It should be kept in mind that material parameters change as concerned frequency change. (More regarding frequency dependent material parameters is provided in sub-section 2.2.1) Hence, the energy loss due to conductivity, which is $(\frac{\sigma}{\omega \epsilon_0})$, is incorporated to the permittivity ϵ.

Now Eq.(2.17) can be written in a scalar manner as follows:

$$\frac{\partial D_x}{\partial t} = \frac{\partial H_z}{\partial z} - \frac{\partial H_y}{\partial x} \quad (2.19)$$

$$\frac{\partial D_y}{\partial t} = \frac{\partial H_x}{\partial z} - \frac{\partial H_z}{\partial x} \quad (2.20)$$

$$\frac{\partial D_z}{\partial t} = \frac{\partial H_y}{\partial x} - \frac{\partial H_x}{\partial y}. \quad (2.21)$$

The equations from Eq.(2.11) to Eq.(2.16), and from Eq.(2.19) to Eq.(2.21), which are provide above, will be used for the computation purpose of Finite-Difference Time-Domain (FDTD) method.

2.2 Finite-Difference Time-Domain (FDTD)

The Finite-Difference Time-Domain (FDTD) method is simple in terms of implementation to solve problems in electromagnetism but the accuracy of the method is contingent upon the implementation. The FDTD method can accurately tackle and solve a wide range of complicated problems, but in general it is computationally expensive.

The FDTD method employs finite differences to find approximate solution of the derivatives that appear in the Maxwell's Equations. Kane Yee in the year 1966 [3] first proposed FDTD algorithm, which employs second-order central differences and the algorithm can be summarized as follows:

Step 1: Replace all the derivatives in Ampere's Law and Faraday's Law with finite differences

Step 2: Discretize space and time in such a way that the electric and magnetic fields are staggered in both space and time

Step 3: Solve the resulting differential equations to obtain "update equation", which express future (unknown) fields in terms of past (known) fields

Step 4: Calculate the magnetic fields one time-step into the future so that they are now known values, which will effectively become past fields

Step 5: Calculate the electric fields one time-step into the future so that they are now known values, which will effectively become past fields

Step 6: Repeat steps 4 and 5 until all the fields have been obtained over the desired time duration

As discussed in the previous section (section 2.1), the time-dependent Maxwell's curl equations (Eq.(2.1), Eq.(2.2)) were originally represented in the finite difference model by Yee. The special arrangement of the unification of electric and magnetic field components proposed by Yee is commonly known as 'Yee Cell' (see Fig.2.1). The distribution of electromagnetic components in Yee Cell assists in solving Maxwell's equations (Eq.(2.1), Eq.(2.2)) in discretized form with second order accuracy. The discretized form of the Maxwell's curl equations are as follows:

Eq.(2.11) is discretized,

$$
\frac{E_z^n(i,j,k) - E_z^n(i,j-1,k)}{\Delta y} - \frac{E_y^n(i,j-\frac{1}{2},k+\frac{1}{2}) - E_y^n(i,j-\frac{1}{2},k-\frac{1}{2})}{\Delta z} =
$$
$$
-\frac{\mu^{n+\frac{1}{2}}(i,j-\frac{1}{2},k) H_x^{n+\frac{1}{2}}(i,j-\frac{1}{2},k) - \mu^{n-\frac{1}{2}}(i,j-\frac{1}{2},k) H_x^{n-\frac{1}{2}}(i,j-\frac{1}{2},k)}{\Delta t}
\tag{2.22}
$$

Eq.(2.12) is discretized,

$$
\frac{E_x^n(i-\frac{1}{2},j,k+\frac{1}{2}) - E_x^n(i-\frac{1}{2},j,k-\frac{1}{2})}{\Delta z} - \frac{E_z^n(i,j,k) - E_z^n(i-1,j,k)}{\Delta x} =
$$
$$
-\frac{\mu^{n+\frac{1}{2}}(i-\frac{1}{2},j,k) H_y^{n+\frac{1}{2}}(i-\frac{1}{2},j,k) - \mu^{n-\frac{1}{2}}(i-\frac{1}{2},j,k) H_y^{n-\frac{1}{2}}(i-\frac{1}{2},j,k)}{\Delta t}
\tag{2.23}
$$

Eq.(2.13) is discretized,

$$\frac{E_y^n{}_{(i,j+\frac{1}{2},k+\frac{1}{2})} - E_y^n{}_{(i-1,j+\frac{1}{2},k+\frac{1}{2})}}{\Delta x} - \frac{E_x^n{}_{(i+\frac{1}{2},j,k+\frac{1}{2})} - E_x^n{}_{(i+\frac{1}{2},j-1,k+\frac{1}{2})}}{\Delta y} = \quad (2.24)$$

$$-\frac{\mu^{n+\frac{1}{2}}{}_{(i-\frac{1}{2},j-\frac{1}{2},k+\frac{1}{2})} H_z^{n+\frac{1}{2}}{}_{(i-\frac{1}{2},j-\frac{1}{2},k+\frac{1}{2})} - \mu^{n-\frac{1}{2}}{}_{(i-\frac{1}{2},j-\frac{1}{2},k+\frac{1}{2})} H_z^{n-\frac{1}{2}}{}_{(i-\frac{1}{2},j-\frac{1}{2},k+\frac{1}{2})}}{\Delta t}$$

Eq.(2.14) is discretized,

$$\frac{H_z^{n-\frac{1}{2}}{}_{(i-\frac{1}{2},j+\frac{1}{2},k+\frac{1}{2})} - H_z^{n-\frac{1}{2}}{}_{(i-\frac{1}{2},j-\frac{1}{2},k+\frac{1}{2})}}{\Delta y} - \frac{H_y^{n-\frac{1}{2}}{}_{(i-\frac{1}{2},j,k+1)} - H_y^{n-\frac{1}{2}}{}_{(i-\frac{1}{2},j,k)}}{\Delta z} = \quad (2.25)$$

$$\frac{\epsilon^n{}_{(i-\frac{1}{2},j,k+\frac{1}{2})} E_x^n{}_{(i-\frac{1}{2},j,k+\frac{1}{2})} - \epsilon^{n-1}{}_{(i-\frac{1}{2},j,k+\frac{1}{2})} E_x^{n-1}{}_{(i-\frac{1}{2},j,k+\frac{1}{2})}}{\Delta t}$$

Eq.(2.15) is discretized

$$\frac{H_x^{n-\frac{1}{2}}{}_{(i,j-\frac{1}{2},k+1)} - H_x^{n-\frac{1}{2}}{}_{(i,j-\frac{1}{2},k)}}{\Delta z} - \frac{H_z^{n-\frac{1}{2}}{}_{(i+\frac{1}{2},j-\frac{1}{2},k+\frac{1}{2})} - H_z^{n-\frac{1}{2}}{}_{(i-\frac{1}{2},j-\frac{1}{2},k+\frac{1}{2})}}{\Delta x} = \quad (2.26)$$

$$\frac{\epsilon^n{}_{(i,j-\frac{1}{2},k+\frac{1}{2})} E_y^n{}_{(i,j-\frac{1}{2},k+\frac{1}{2})} - \epsilon^{n-1}{}_{(i,j-\frac{1}{2},k+\frac{1}{2})} E_y^{n-1}{}_{(i,j-\frac{1}{2},k+\frac{1}{2})}}{\Delta t}$$

Eq.(2.16) is discretized,

$$\frac{H_y^{n-\frac{1}{2}}{}_{(i+\frac{1}{2},j,k)} - H_y^{n-\frac{1}{2}}{}_{(i-\frac{1}{2},j,k)}}{\Delta x} - \frac{H_x^{n-\frac{1}{2}}{}_{(i,j+\frac{1}{2},k)} - H_x^{n-\frac{1}{2}}{}_{(i,j-\frac{1}{2},k)}}{\Delta y} = \quad (2.27)$$

$$\frac{\epsilon^n{}_{(i,j,k)} E_z^n{}_{(i,j,k)} - \epsilon^{n-1}{}_{(i,j,k)} E_z^{n-1}{}_{(i,j,k)}}{\Delta t}$$

where, Δt is time step, n is time step index, Δx, Δy, Δz are Yee cell dimensions, and (i, j, k) are Yee cell indices.

This set of discretized equations (Eq.(2.22) - Eq.(2.27)) forms the basis of finite-difference time-domain (FDTD) computation. From the equations it should be noticed that the electric and magnetic field components are computed in consecutive time intervals, which is half of time step Δt, and is commonly known as 'leapfrog time-stepping' technique.

Using the equations from Eq.(2.22) - Eq.(2.27) explicit finite difference equations are defined, which are the 'update equations' as mentioned in Yee's algorithm. [1] The finite difference equations are as follows.

---

[1] The finite difference equations are calculated when the origins of $E_x(0,0,0)$, $E_y(0,0,0)$, $E_z(0,0,0)$, $H_x(0,0,0)$, $H_y(0,0,0)$ and $H_z(0,0,0)$ are placed in Cartesian coordinates as shown in Yee Cell (Fig.2.1)

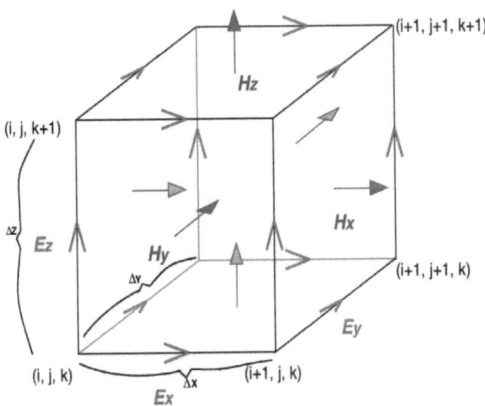

Figure 2.1: Yee Cell, representing Yee's algorithm regarding electromagnetic fields in three dimensional space. Magnetic field is perpendicular to the surface on which electric field acts. The fields (electric and magnetic) follow each other alternatively and because of this interleaving, the magnetic field and the electric field are co-dependent.

Equation Eq.(2.22) generates:

$$\frac{E_z^n{}_{(i,j+1,k)} - E_z^n{}_{(i,j,k)}}{\Delta y} - \frac{E_y^n{}_{(i,j,k+1)} - E_y^n{}_{(i,j,k)}}{\Delta z} = \tag{2.28}$$

$$-\frac{\mu^n{}_{(i,j,k)} H_x^n{}_{(i,j,k)} - \mu^{n-1}{}_{(i,j,k)} H_x^{n-1}{}_{(i,j,k)}}{\Delta t}$$

$$\therefore H_x^n{}_{(i,j,k)} = \frac{\mu^{n-1}{}_{(i,j,k)} H_x^{n-1}{}_{(i,j,k)}}{\mu^n{}_{(i,j,k)}}$$

$$-\frac{\Delta t}{\mu^n{}_{(i,j,k)}} \left[\frac{E_z^n{}_{(i,j+1,k)} - E_z^n{}_{(i,j,k)}}{\Delta y} - \frac{E_y^n{}_{(i,j,k+1)} - E_y^n{}_{(i,j,k)}}{\Delta z} \right]$$

$$, [i_{min} + 1 \leq i \leq i_{max} - 1, j_{min} + 1 \leq j \leq j_{max}, k_{min} + 1 \leq k \leq k_{max}].$$

Equation Eq.(2.23) yields:

$$\frac{E_x^n{}_{(i,j,k+1)} - E_x^n{}_{(i,j,k)}}{\Delta z} - \frac{E_z^n{}_{(i+1,j,k)} - E_z^n{}_{(i,j,k)}}{\Delta x} = \tag{2.29}$$

$$-\frac{\mu^n{}_{(i,j,k)} H_y^n{}_{(i,j,k)} - \mu^{n-1}{}_{(i,j,k)} H_y^{n-1}{}_{(i,j,k)}}{\Delta t}$$

$$\therefore H_y^n{}_{(i,j,k)} = \frac{\mu^{n-1}{}_{(i,j,k)} H_y^{n-1}{}_{(i,j,k)}}{\mu^n{}_{(i,j,k)}}$$

$$-\frac{\Delta t}{\mu^n{}_{(i,j,k)}}\left[\frac{E_x^n{}_{(i,j,k+1)} - E_x^n{}_{(i,j,k)}}{\Delta z} - \frac{E_z^n{}_{(i+1,j,k)} - E_z^n{}_{(i,j,k)}}{\Delta x}\right]$$
$$, [i_{min} + 1 \le i \le i_{max}, j_{min} + 1 \le j \le j_{max} - 1, k_{min} + 1 \le k \le k_{max}].$$

Equation Eq.(2.24) forms:

$$\frac{E_y^n{}_{(i+1,j,k)} - E_y^n{}_{(i,j,k)}}{\Delta x} - \frac{E_x^n{}_{(i,j+1,k)} - E_x^n{}_{(i,j,k)}}{\Delta y} = \tag{2.30}$$
$$-\frac{\mu^n{}_{(i,j,k)} H_z^n{}_{(i,j,k)} - \mu^{n-1}{}_{(i,j,k)} H_z^{n-1}{}_{(i,j,k)}}{\Delta t}$$
$$\therefore H_z^n{}_{(i,j,k)} = \frac{\mu^{n-1}{}_{(i,j,k)} H_z^{n-1}{}_{(i,j,k)}}{\mu^n{}_{(i,j,k)}}$$
$$-\frac{\Delta t}{\mu^n{}_{(i,j,k)}}\left[\frac{E_y^n{}_{(i+1,j,k)} - E_y^n{}_{(i,j,k)}}{\Delta x} - \frac{E_x^n{}_{(i,j+1,k)} - E_x^n{}_{(i,j,k)}}{\Delta y}\right]$$
$$, [i_{min} + 1 \le i \le i_{max}, j_{min} + 1 \le j \le j_{max}, k_{min} + 1 \le k \le k_{max} - 1].$$

Equation Eq.(2.25) is simplified to:

$$\frac{H_z^n{}_{(i,j+1,k)} - H_z^n{}_{(i,j,k)}}{\Delta y} - \frac{H_y^n{}_{(i,j,k+1)} - H_y^n{}_{(i,j,k)}}{\Delta z} = \tag{2.31}$$
$$\frac{\epsilon^{n+1}{}_{(i,j,k)} E_x^{n+1}{}_{(i,j,k)} - \epsilon^n{}_{(i,j,k)} E_x^n{}_{(i,j,k)}}{\Delta t}$$
$$\therefore E_x^{n+1}{}_{(i,j,k)} = \frac{\epsilon^n{}_{(i,j,k)} E_x^n{}_{(i,j,k)}}{\epsilon^{n+1}{}_{(i,j,k)}}$$
$$+\frac{\Delta t}{\epsilon^{n+1}{}_{(i,j,k)}}\left[\frac{H_z^n{}_{(i,j+1,k)} - H_z^n{}_{(i,j,k)}}{\Delta y} - \frac{H_y^n{}_{(i,j,k+1)} - H_y^n{}_{(i,j,k)}}{\Delta z}\right]$$
$$, [i_{min} + 1 \le i \le i_{max}, j_{min} \le j \le j_{max}, k_{min} \le k \le k_{max}].$$

Equation Eq.(2.26) generates:

$$\frac{H_x^n{}_{(i,j,k+1)} - H_x^n{}_{(i,j,k)}}{\Delta z} - \frac{H_z^n{}_{(i+1,j,k)} - H_z^n{}_{(i,j,k)}}{\Delta x} = \tag{2.32}$$
$$\frac{\epsilon^{n+1}{}_{(i,j,k)} E_y^{n+1}{}_{(i,j,k)} - \epsilon^n{}_{(i,j,k)} E_y^n{}_{(i,j,k)}}{\Delta t}$$
$$\therefore E_y^{n+1}{}_{(i,j,k)} = \frac{\epsilon^n{}_{(i,j,k)} E_y^n{}_{(i,j,k)}}{\epsilon^{n+1}{}_{(i,j,k)}}$$
$$+\frac{\Delta t}{\epsilon^{n+1}{}_{(i,j,k)}}\left[\frac{H_x^n{}_{(i,j,k+1)} - H_x^n{}_{(i,j,k)}}{\Delta z} - \frac{H_z^n{}_{(i+1,j,k)} - H_z^n{}_{(i,j,k)}}{\Delta x}\right]$$
$$, [i_{min} \le i \le i_{max}, j_{min} + 1 \le j \le j_{max}, k_{min} \le k \le k_{max}].$$

Equation Eq.(2.27) is also simplified to:

$$\frac{H_y^n(i+1,j,k) - H_y^n(i,j,k)}{\Delta x} - \frac{H_x^n(i,j+1,k) - H_x^n(i,j,k)}{\Delta y} = \quad (2.33)$$

$$\frac{\epsilon^{n+1}(i,j,k) E_z^{n+1}(i,j,k) - \epsilon^n(i,j,k) E_z^n(i,j,k)}{\Delta t}$$

$$\therefore E_z^{n+1}(i,j,k) = \frac{\epsilon^n(i,j,k) E_z^n(i,j,k)}{\epsilon^{n+1}(i,j,k)}$$

$$+ \frac{\Delta t}{\epsilon^{n+1}(i,j,k)} \left[\frac{H_y^n(i+1,j,k) - H_y^n(i,j,k)}{\Delta x} - \frac{H_x^n(i,j+1,k) - H_x^n(i,j,k)}{\Delta y} \right]$$

$$, [i_{min} \leq i \leq i_{max}, j_{min} \leq j \leq j_{max}, k_{min} + 1 \leq k \leq k_{max}]$$

In the above equations, $E_x^n(i,j_{min},k)$, $E_x^n(i,j_{max},k)$, $E_x^n(i,j,k_{min})$, $E_x^n(i,j,k_{max})$, $E_y^n(i_{min},j,k)$, $E_y^n(i_{max},j,k)$, $E_y^n(i,j,k_{min})$, $E_y^n(i,j,k_{max})$, $E_z^n(i_{min},j,k)$, $E_z^n(i_{max},j,k)$, $E_z^n(i,j_{min},k)$, $E_z^n(i,j_{max},k)$ are calculated by the 'boundary condition', which is discussed later in 2.2.2. The equations from Eq.(2.28) to Eq.(2.33) are explicitly used by FDTD method along with the boundary condition to form the update equations for H (magnetic field) and E (electric field).

If source free environment is considered then it is also possible to calculate D (electric flux) as follows.

Equation Eq.(2.2) is re-written as:

$$\frac{H_z^n(i,j,k) - H_z^n(i,j-1,k)}{\Delta y} - \frac{H_y^n(i,j,k) - H_y^n(i,j,k-1)}{\Delta z} = \quad (2.34)$$

$$\frac{D_x^{n+1}(i,j,k) - D_x^n(i,j,k)}{\Delta t}$$

$$\therefore D_x^{n+1}(i,j,k) =$$

$$\Delta t \left[\frac{H_z^n(i,j,k) - H_z^n(i,j-1,k)}{\Delta y} - \frac{H_y^n(i,j,k) - H_y^n(i,j,k-1)}{\Delta z} \right] + D_x^n(i,j,k)$$

$$, [i_{min} + 1 \leq i \leq i_{max}, j_{min} \leq j \leq j_{max}, k_{min} \leq k \leq k_{max}]$$

$$\frac{H_x^n(i,j,k) - H_x^n(i,j,k-1)}{\Delta z} - \frac{H_z^n(i,j,k) - H_z^n(i-1,j,k)}{\Delta x} = \quad (2.35)$$

$$\frac{D_y^{n+1}(i,j,k) - D_y^n(i,j,k)}{\Delta t}$$

$$\therefore D_y^{n+1}(i,j,k) =$$

$$\Delta t \left[\frac{H_x^n(i,j,k) - H_x^n(i,j,k-1)}{\Delta z} - \frac{H_z^n(i,j,k) - H_z^n(i-1,j,k)}{\Delta x} \right] + D_y^n(i,j,k)$$

$$, [i_{min} \leq i \leq i_{max}, j_{min} + 1 \leq j \leq j_{max}, k_{min} \leq k \leq k_{max}]$$

$$\frac{H_y^n{}_{(i,j,k)} - H_y^n{}_{(i-1,j,k)}}{\Delta x} - \frac{H_x^n{}_{(i,j,k)} - H_x^n{}_{(i,j-1,k)}}{\Delta y} = \tag{2.36}$$

$$\frac{D_z^{n+1}{}_{(i,j,k)} - D_z^n{}_{(i,j,k)}}{\Delta t}$$

$$\therefore D_z^{n+1}{}_{(i,j,k)} =$$

$$\Delta t \left[\frac{H_y^n{}_{(i,j,k)} - H_y^n{}_{(i-1,j,k)}}{\Delta x} - \frac{H_x^n{}_{(i,j,k)} - H_x^n{}_{(i,j-1,k)}}{\Delta y} \right] + D_z^n{}_{(i,j,k)}$$

$$, [i_{min} \leq i \leq i_{max}, j_{min} \leq j \leq j_{max}, k_{min} + 1 \leq k \leq k_{max}].$$

2.2.1 Frequency Dependent Material Parameters & Frequency Dependent FDTD

Now, from equation Eq.(2.17), the energy loss ($\frac{\sigma}{\omega\epsilon_0}$) due to conductivity is known as the 'ionic-conductive loss'. At low frequency, the energy loss is relatively high due to this. The ability of a material to be polarised by the external electric field is called 'relative permittivity'. The efficiency with which the electromagnetic energy is converted to heat is represented as 'Loss Tangent' ($\tan\delta$). When the relative permittivity (ϵ_r) is real number, loss tangent can be represented mathematically as:

$$\tan\delta = \frac{\sigma}{\omega\epsilon_0\epsilon_r}. \tag{2.37}$$

According to Costen [21] in linear classical electrodynamics the materials, which exhibits the effects of dispersion [2], are characterised as either of the three: Debye type materials or Lorentz type materials or based on the Cole-Cole Circular Arc law. According to [21]:

> "The Debye type is appropriate for polar liquids in the microwave regime
> and this type is due to the rotational motion of the molecules. The
> Lorentz model is based on the motion of bounded charges and leads to
> a system with a couple of resonant frequencies."

---

[2]Dispersive Materials that exhibit the effect of dispersion in that medium based on the properties of the wave traveling within that medium. One example is refraction of a light in a prism is due to dispersion

Since, most of the papers, which deal with the dispersive materials in Finite Difference Time Domain method (FDTD), have used the Debye Model, therefore this thesis also adopts the most poplar Debye model for the dispersive materials. Peter J. W. Debye [22] generalised the behaviour of materials with orientational polarisability in a relaxed dielectric polarization region. When the applied frequency is much lower than the high visible frequencies ($4 \times 10^{14} \sim 8 \times 10^{14}$ Hz) the relative permittivity is referred to as the static relative dielectric constant (static permittivity) and denoted by ϵ_S. And for much greater frequencies, the relative permittivity is referred to as the infinite relative dielectric constant ϵ_∞ (optical permittivity). Intermediate relative permittivity is denoted by ϵ_m.

Now if Debye model is considered then the relative permittivity can be represented as a complex number of first order and second order respectively as:

First Order Debye Model:

$$\epsilon_r = \epsilon_\infty + \frac{\epsilon_S - \epsilon_\infty}{1 + \jmath\omega\tau_D} \tag{2.38}$$

Second Order Debye Model:

$$\epsilon_r = \epsilon_\infty + \frac{\epsilon_S - \epsilon_m}{1 + \jmath\omega\tau_D} + \frac{\epsilon_m - \epsilon_\infty}{1 + \jmath\omega\tau_2} \tag{2.39}$$

where, τ_D is the characteristic relaxation time of the dipole moment of the molecules , which is a time constant and the polarization decays exponentially with this time constant, as assumed by Debye. And τ_2 is relatively a short relaxation time.

The permittivity is expressed in the following way using the first oder Debye model:

$$
\begin{aligned}
\epsilon &= \epsilon_0 \left(\epsilon_\infty + \frac{\epsilon_S - \epsilon_\infty}{1 + \jmath\omega\tau_D} - \jmath\frac{\sigma}{\omega\epsilon_0} \right) \\
&= \epsilon_0 \left(\epsilon_\infty + \frac{\epsilon_S - \epsilon_\infty}{1 + (\omega\tau_D)^2} - \jmath\{ \frac{\sigma}{\omega\epsilon_0} + \frac{\omega\tau_D(\epsilon_S - \epsilon_\infty)}{1 + (\omega\tau_D)^2} \} \right).
\end{aligned} \tag{2.40}
$$

Here, the imaginary part of relative permittivity, ϵ_r , which is, $(\frac{\omega\tau_D(\epsilon_S - \epsilon_\infty)}{1 + (\omega\tau_D)^2})$, is called the 'dielectric loss'.

Now from the equations Eq.(2.6) and Eq.(2.40) the following equation can be formed:

$$\boldsymbol{D} = \left(\epsilon_0\epsilon_\infty + \frac{\epsilon_0\epsilon_S - \epsilon_0\epsilon_\infty}{1 + \jmath\omega\tau_D} - \jmath\frac{\sigma}{\omega}\right)\boldsymbol{E} \tag{2.41}$$

$$= \left(\epsilon_0\epsilon_\infty + \frac{\epsilon_0\epsilon_S - \epsilon_0\epsilon_\infty}{1 + \jmath\omega\tau_D} + \frac{\sigma}{\jmath\omega}\right)\boldsymbol{E}$$

$$= \frac{(\jmath\omega)^2\epsilon_0\epsilon_\infty\tau_D + \jmath\omega(\epsilon_0\epsilon_S + \sigma\tau_D) + \sigma}{\jmath\omega(1 + \jmath\omega\tau_D)}\boldsymbol{E}.$$

The above equation (Eq.(2.41)) can be rewritten as:

$$(\jmath\omega)^2\tau_D\boldsymbol{D} + (\jmath\omega)\boldsymbol{D} = (\jmath\omega)^2\epsilon_0\epsilon_\infty\tau_D\boldsymbol{E} + \jmath\omega(\epsilon_0\epsilon_S + \sigma\tau_D)\boldsymbol{E} + \sigma\boldsymbol{E}. \tag{2.42}$$

If the time-dependency is assumed to be $\exp(\jmath\omega t)$, then Eq.(2.42) can be expressed as a differential equation in time domain in the following way:

$$\frac{\partial^2(\tau_D\boldsymbol{D})}{\partial t^2} + \frac{\partial\boldsymbol{D}}{\partial t} = \frac{\partial^2(\epsilon_0\epsilon_\infty\tau_D\boldsymbol{E})}{\partial t^2} + \frac{\partial(\epsilon_0\epsilon_S + \sigma\tau_D)\boldsymbol{E}}{\partial t} + \sigma\boldsymbol{E}. \tag{2.43}$$

Eq.(2.43) can be expressed in the difference form if the environment does not change with time, and can be written as:

$$\tau_D\frac{D_z^{n+1}{}_{(i,j,k)} - 2D_z^n{}_{(i,j,k)} + D_z^{n-1}{}_{(i,j,k)}}{(\Delta t)^2} + \frac{D_z^{n+1}{}_{(i,j,k)} - D_z^n{}_{(i,j,k)}}{\Delta t} = \tag{2.44}$$

$$\epsilon_0\epsilon_\infty\tau_D\frac{E_z^{n+1}{}_{(i,j,k)} - 2E_z^n{}_{(i,j,k)} + E_z^{n-1}{}_{(i,j,k)}}{(\Delta t)^2} +$$

$$(\epsilon_0\epsilon_S + \sigma\tau_D)\frac{E_z^{n+1}{}_{(i,j,k)} - E_z^n{}_{(i,j,k)}}{\Delta t} + \sigma\frac{E_z^{n+1}{}_{(i,j,k)} + E_z^n{}_{(i,j,k)}}{2}.$$

The above equation (Eq.(2.44)) is corresponding the calculation of $E_z^{n+1}{}_{(i,j,k)}$. $E_x^{n+1}{}_{(i,j,k)}$ or $E_y^{n+1}{}_{(i,j,k)}$ can be calculated just by replacing the "z" by "x" or "y" respectively. Again, if the environment does change with time then Eq.(2.43) can be written in the following difference forms:

$$E_x^{n+1}{}_{(i,j,k)} = \frac{-\sigma^n(\Delta t)^2 + 4\epsilon_0\epsilon_\infty^n\tau_D^n + 2(\epsilon_0\epsilon_S^n + \sigma^n\tau_D^n)\Delta t}{2\epsilon_0\epsilon_\infty^{n+1}\tau_D^{n+1} + 2(\epsilon_0\epsilon_S^{n+1} + \sigma^{n+1}\tau_D^{n+1})\Delta t + \sigma^{n+1}(\Delta t)^2}E_x^n{}_{(i,j,k)} \tag{2.45}$$

$$-\frac{2\epsilon_0\epsilon_\infty^{n-1}\tau_D^{n-1}}{2\epsilon_0\epsilon_\infty^{n+1}\tau_D^{n+1} + 2(\epsilon_0\epsilon_S^{n+1} + \sigma^{n+1}\tau_D^{n+1})\Delta t + \sigma^{n+1}(\Delta t)^2}E_x^{n-1}{}_{(i,j,k)}$$

$$+\frac{2(\Delta t + \tau_D^{n+1})}{2\epsilon_0\epsilon_\infty^{n+1}\tau_D^{n+1} + 2(\epsilon_0\epsilon_S^{n+1} + \sigma^{n+1}\tau_D^{n+1})\Delta t + \sigma^{n+1}(\Delta t)^2}D_x^{n+1}{}_{(i,j,k)}$$

$$-\frac{2\Delta t + 4\tau_{\mathrm{D}}^n}{2\epsilon_0\epsilon_\infty^{n+1}\tau_{\mathrm{D}}^{n+1} + 2(\epsilon_0\epsilon_{\mathrm{S}}^{n+1} + \sigma^{n+1}\tau_{\mathrm{D}}^{n+1})\Delta t + \sigma^{n+1}(\Delta t)^2}D_x^n{}_{(i,j,k)}$$

$$+\frac{2\tau_{\mathrm{D}}^{n-1}}{2\epsilon_0\epsilon_\infty^{n+1}\tau_{\mathrm{D}}^{n+1} + 2(\epsilon_0\epsilon_{\mathrm{S}}^{n+1} + \sigma^{n+1}\tau_{\mathrm{D}}^{n+1})\Delta t + \sigma^{n+1}(\Delta t)^2}D_x^{n-1}{}_{(i,j,k)}.$$

$$E_y^{n+1}{}_{(i,j,k)} = \frac{-\sigma^n(\Delta t)^2 + 4\epsilon_0\epsilon_\infty^n\tau_{\mathrm{D}}^n + 2(\epsilon_0\epsilon_{\mathrm{S}}^n + \sigma^n\tau_{\mathrm{D}}^n)\Delta t}{2\epsilon_0\epsilon_\infty^{n+1}\tau_{\mathrm{D}}^{n+1} + 2(\epsilon_0\epsilon_{\mathrm{S}}^{n+1} + \sigma^{n+1}\tau_{\mathrm{D}}^{n+1})\Delta t + \sigma^{n+1}(\Delta t)^2}E_y^n{}_{(i,j,k)} \quad (2.46)$$

$$-\frac{2\epsilon_0\epsilon_\infty^{n-1}\tau_{\mathrm{D}}^{n-1}}{2\epsilon_0\epsilon_\infty^{n+1}\tau_{\mathrm{D}}^{n+1} + 2(\epsilon_0\epsilon_{\mathrm{S}}^{n+1} + \sigma^{n+1}\tau_{\mathrm{D}}^{n+1})\Delta t + \sigma^{n+1}(\Delta t)^2}E_y^{n-1}{}_{(i,j,k)}$$

$$+\frac{2(\Delta t + \tau_{\mathrm{D}}^{n+1})}{2\epsilon_0\epsilon_\infty^{n+1}\tau_{\mathrm{D}}^{n+1} + 2(\epsilon_0\epsilon_{\mathrm{S}}^{n+1} + \sigma^{n+1}\tau_{\mathrm{D}}^{n+1})\Delta t + \sigma^{n+1}(\Delta t)^2}D_y^{n+1}{}_{(i,j,k)}$$

$$-\frac{2\Delta t + 4\tau_{\mathrm{D}}^n}{2\epsilon_0\epsilon_\infty^{n+1}\tau_{\mathrm{D}}^{n+1} + 2(\epsilon_0\epsilon_{\mathrm{S}}^{n+1} + \sigma^{n+1}\tau_{\mathrm{D}}^{n+1})\Delta t + \sigma^{n+1}(\Delta t)^2}D_y^n{}_{(i,j,k)}$$

$$+\frac{2\tau_{\mathrm{D}}^{n-1}}{2\epsilon_0\epsilon_\infty^{n+1}\tau_{\mathrm{D}}^{n+1} + 2(\epsilon_0\epsilon_{\mathrm{S}}^{n+1} + \sigma^{n+1}\tau_{\mathrm{D}}^{n+1})\Delta t + \sigma^{n+1}(\Delta t)^2}D_y^{n-1}{}_{(i,j,k)}.$$

$$E_z^{n+1}{}_{(i,j,k)} = \frac{-\sigma^n(\Delta t)^2 + 4\epsilon_0\epsilon_\infty^n\tau_{\mathrm{D}}^n + 2(\epsilon_0\epsilon_{\mathrm{S}}^n + \sigma^n\tau_{\mathrm{D}}^n)\Delta t}{2\epsilon_0\epsilon_\infty^{n+1}\tau_{\mathrm{D}}^{n+1} + 2(\epsilon_0\epsilon_{\mathrm{S}}^{n+1} + \sigma^{n+1}\tau_{\mathrm{D}}^{n+1})\Delta t + \sigma^{n+1}(\Delta t)^2}E_z^n{}_{(i,j,k)} \quad (2.47)$$

$$-\frac{2\epsilon_0\epsilon_\infty^{n-1}\tau_{\mathrm{D}}^{n-1}}{2\epsilon_0\epsilon_\infty^{n+1}\tau_{\mathrm{D}}^{n+1} + 2(\epsilon_0\epsilon_{\mathrm{S}}^{n+1} + \sigma^{n+1}\tau_{\mathrm{D}}^{n+1})\Delta t + \sigma^{n+1}(\Delta t)^2}E_z^{n-1}{}_{(i,j,k)}$$

$$+\frac{2(\Delta t + \tau_{\mathrm{D}}^{n+1})}{2\epsilon_0\epsilon_\infty^{n+1}\tau_{\mathrm{D}}^{n+1} + 2(\epsilon_0\epsilon_{\mathrm{S}}^{n+1} + \sigma^{n+1}\tau_{\mathrm{D}}^{n+1})\Delta t + \sigma^{n+1}(\Delta t)^2}D_z^{n+1}{}_{(i,j,k)}$$

$$-\frac{2\Delta t + 4\tau_{\mathrm{D}}^n}{2\epsilon_0\epsilon_\infty^{n+1}\tau_{\mathrm{D}}^{n+1} + 2(\epsilon_0\epsilon_{\mathrm{S}}^{n+1} + \sigma^{n+1}\tau_{\mathrm{D}}^{n+1})\Delta t + \sigma^{n+1}(\Delta t)^2}D_z^n{}_{(i,j,k)}$$

$$+\frac{2\tau_{\mathrm{D}}^{n-1}}{2\epsilon_0\epsilon_\infty^{n+1}\tau_{\mathrm{D}}^{n+1} + 2(\epsilon_0\epsilon_{\mathrm{S}}^{n+1} + \sigma^{n+1}\tau_{\mathrm{D}}^{n+1})\Delta t + \sigma^{n+1}(\Delta t)^2}D_z^{n-1}{}_{(i,j,k)}.$$

Therefore, equations Eq.(2.45), Eq.(2.46), Eq.(2.47) are utilized to calculate E from D.

2.2.2 Boundary Condition

Many Yee cell together in a grid constitutes a mesh (see Fig.2.2). In the equations Eq.(2.28) - Eq.(2.33), the H is calculated using the update equations where the H field vector components are internal to the mesh. It is to be noted that the normal H components on the faces of the mesh are never used to update any other field values and the normal vectors on the faces of the mesh are never calculated. If the mesh and

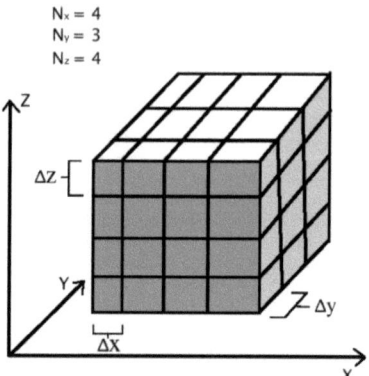

Figure 2.2: An Example of Orthogonal Mesh, with $[i, j, k]$ indices where $i = 0, 1, 2,...,$ Nx; $j = 0, 1, 2,..., Ny$; $k = 0, 1, 2,..., Nz$

the aforementioned equations are taken into consideration then it can be noticed that to calculate H, every H field component requires the values of the four surrounding co-plane E field (See the Fig.2.3), and every E field component requires the four surrounding H values on the two planes to which it belongs (See the Fig.2.4). Now, it can be noticed from Fig.2.5 that some E values on the outer cells of the mesh/grid i.e. the cells that make the outer faces, can not be calculated because there are some missing H values. Therefore the field components, which can not be calculated because of the missing values of few other field components, will require Absorbing Boundary Conditions (ABCs) to be calculated using FDTD.

In FDTD, values of every field components are calculated only at discrete points. To approximate Maxwell's equations using finite differences, one equation for every field component at every discrete point on the mesh is generated. To calculate field components at the edge of the mesh, the inclusion of a field component outside the grid is necessary but in reality it does not exists. The method by which this problem can be handled is called a boundary condition.

Now, due to limited amount of memory in computers the calculation can not be infinite and for this reason one of the major challenges of using FDTD method is the mesh

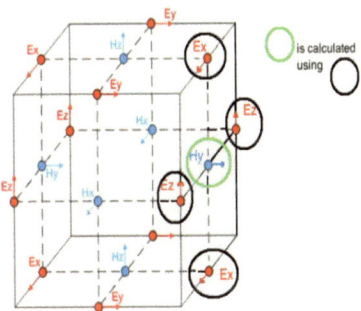

Figure 2.3: Yee Cell where H field component requires the values of four surrounding co-plane E field

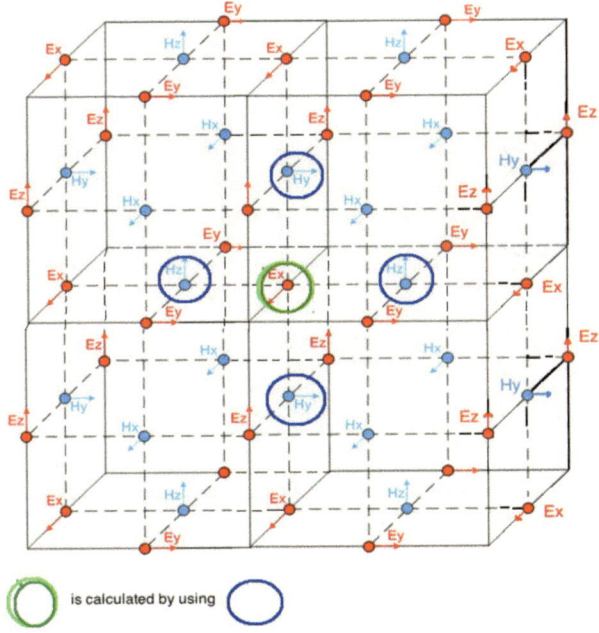

Figure 2.4: Mesh where E field component requires the four surrounding H values on the two planes to which it belongs

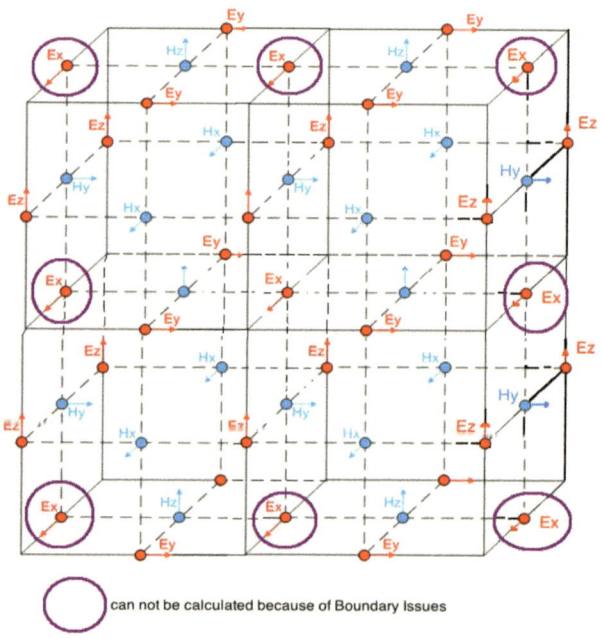

Figure 2.5: Some components can not be calculated because of the boundary issues

truncation method. In reality a truncation method which shows better accuracy may experience lower stability and vice-versa. Therefore the area, where the calculations are performed, is terminated either by reflecting the waves perfectly or by absorbing the waves without reflection. One of the popular, Dirichlet boundary conditions [23–27], assume that the fields outside the grid are all zero. When the fields are forced to be zero outside the grid, it means that outside of the grid is either a "Perfect Electric Conductor" or a "Perfect Magnetic Conductor", depending on what field type is forced to be zero. This is the case when the waves are reflected perfectly. In reality, "Perfect Electric Conductor" or "Perfect Magnetic Conductor" is not possible to achieve in all circumstances and hence this method will not be the focus for this thesis. Again according to [21], there are a wide range of non-reflecting boundary conditions but most of them are either classified as a 'damping zone method' or a 'radiating boundary method', but depends on the one way wave equation.

Damping zone methods such as the Perfectly Matched Layer (PML) Absorbing Boundary Condition (ABC) are good in increasing accuracy by reducing the strength of the wave over a grid/mesh region near the boundary. Methods [28–30] other than PML ABC are flexible and have simple construction procedures. These methods also have relatively small data storage requirements. Therefore for this thesis the considered ABC is based on one way wave equations with a focus on easy construction for inhomogeneous environment, stability, accuracy and less memory requirement unlike other methods available.

2.3 Summary of Maxwell's Equations and FDTD Method

This section summarises sections 2.1 and 2.2 as follows.

1. James C. Maxwell proposed a set of 20 differential equations to relate all electric and magnetic components together

2. Equations from Eq.(2.1) to Eq.(2.5) are the most relevant Maxwell's equations.

3. The FDTD method is a numerical analysis technique, which employs finite differences to find approximate solution of the derivatives that appear in the Maxwell's Equations.

4. According to Kan Yee [3], H and E are calculated using the 'update equations'

5. Equations Eq.(2.28), Eq.(2.29), and Eq.(2.30) are used to calculate H from E

6. Equations Eq.(2.34), Eq.(2.35), and Eq.(2.36) are usued to calculate D from H

7. Equations Eq.(2.45), Eq.(2.46) and Eq.(2.47) are used to calculate E from D

2.4 Computer Implementation of FDTD Method

This section deals with the process of writing the computer-program to compute the aforementioned FDTD method. The computer-program for this thesis was written in FORTRAN (version FORTRAN 90) computer language. It is advisable to get to know about few key points regarding Fortran language before understanding the actual implementation of the FDTD method in computers. It was taken into consideration that the readers of this thesis are aware of basic programming concepts, which will aid them to understand the context provided in this section.

2.4.1 Basics of FORTRAN 90 Programming

A program written in Fortran language has the following basic structure:

```
!This is a basic FORTRAN program structure
PROGRAM program-name
IMPLICIT NONE
[specification-part]
[execution-part]
[subprogram-part]
END PROGRAM program-name


!Basic Structure of a subprogram in Fortran
type FUNCTION function-name (arg1, arg2, ..., argN)
IMPLICIT NONE
[specification part]
[execution part]
[subprogram part]
END FUNCTION function-name
```

In the aforementioned program structure, in the [specification-part] the variables or few other specific things, which are necessary for the computation/calculation part later in the program, are declared; in the [execution-part] the main calculation or the execution of the solution is provided, and in the [subprogram-part] some mini functions/programs, which aids the main program in computation of the solution, are provided. It should be noted that '!' is used to comment anything in Fortran language. The "IMPLICIT NONE" statement forces the programmer to declare all variables after it and is considered to be a good programming style. The 'type' in the subprogram part is the return type of the function subprogram such as integer, real, etc., and the arg1, arg2,...,argN are the fomral arguements or parameters passed to the subprogram.

Refer to the following simple program to calculate area of a rectangle to get an idea reagrding how to write a basic Fortran program.

```
!A simple program to calculate
!are of a rectangle
PROGRAM calculateArea
IMPLICIT NONE
REAL, PARAMETER :: length=6.00, width=12.00, area
area=length*width
write (*,*) "The Area of the Rectangle =", area
END PROGRAM calculateArea
```

To write a program in Fortran to compute FDTD algorithm, it is important to know the cocnept and usage of Arrays in this language. Arrays in Fortran are used to store lists of data, which are all of the same type. Knowing the proper usage of arrays in Fortran will provide good and stable performance of the program implmenting FDTD method because the varibales such as electric field components, magnetic field components, etc., are all stored in array format in the program.

Example of arrays in Fortran:

```
REAL, DIMENSION(10) :: C, D
REAL, DIMENSION(6,20) :: X
DOUBLE PRECISION, DIMENSION(2,3) :: A, B
INTEGER, DIMENSION(24) :: Numbers
```

In the above example, C is a 1-D real type array consisting of 10 elements starting from C(1) to C(10), and is same for D. Whereas, X is a 2-D real type array consisting of 6 X 20 elements, which can be visualised in a matrix format. Again, Numbers is a 1-D array, consisting of 24 integer type elements. It should be kept in mind that arrays in Fortran uses column-major order [3] to store multidimensional arrays in the memory of the computer.

2.4.2 Implementation of FDTD Method

First, to write a program to implement the FDTD method, the input parameters have to be set properly in the following way:

```
!------------------------------------------------------------------
!    Declaring the field values
!------------------------------------------------------------------
        !E (Electric) Field values
        REAL, DIMENSION(:,:,:), ALLOCATABLE :: ex1,ex2,ex3
        REAL, DIMENSION(:,:,:), ALLOCATABLE :: ey1,ey2,ey3
        REAL, DIMENSION(:,:,:), ALLOCATABLE :: ez1,ez2,ez3

        !H (Magnetic) Field Values
        REAL, DIMENSION(:,:,:), ALLOCATABLE :: hx
        REAL, DIMENSION(:,:,:), ALLOCATABLE :: hy
        REAL, DIMENSION(:,:,:), ALLOCATABLE :: hz

        !Values for D (Electric Flux)
        REAL, DIMENSION(:,:,:), ALLOCATABLE :: dx1,dx2,dx3
        REAL, DIMENSION(:,:,:), ALLOCATABLE :: dy1,dy2,dy3
        REAL, DIMENSION(:,:,:), ALLOCATABLE :: dz1,dz2,dz3
```

In the above snippet of code, only the delcaration of few of the field variables are shown in order to give an idea of how to set the parameters, which are necessary for the computation of FDTD algorithm. It should be noticed from the above code snippet that the field components are declared as 3-D array with allocatable option, where memory storage can be assigned during execution. Using an allocatable array provides more flexibility to the programmer to change the number of elements during the execution of program. This also provides a better chance of tracking error. Thus in order to assign memory storage to the declared variables it can be done as following:

---

[3]In computer programming, row-major order and column-major order explains the methods of storing multidimensional arrays in linear memory of the computer. Eg.: Row-major order is used in C/C++, Python, etc., whereas Column-major order is used in Fortran, OpenGL, R, etc.

```
! ------------------------------------------------------------------
!    Allocate field arrays
! ------------------------------------------------------------------
       allocate(ex1(1:nx, 1:ny, 1:nz), stat=err)
       allocate(ex2(1:nx, 1:ny, 1:nz), stat=err)
       allocate(ex3(1:nx, 1:ny, 1:nz), stat=err)
!Where, nx, ny, nz are
!number of elements in each direction.
!stat is the status of aloocation option.
!stat takes the value 0 if allocation is successful
!or some other machine dependent value if the machine
!has insufficient memory to allocate.
```

Now, from section 2.2 it was noticed that there are nine equations (Eq.(2.28) -
Eq.(2.30), Eq.(2.34) - Eq.(2.36), Eq.(2.45) - Eq.(2.47)), which are the most important
for FDTD computation, and these equations have to be calculated in the computer
program. In the example code snippet below it is shown how to implement an update
equation for H_x i.e. magentic field component in X axis.

```
! ------------------------------------------------------------------
!    Updating Hx
! ------------------------------------------------------------------

       do k=1,nz-1
          do j=1,ny-1
             do i=2,nx-1

                hx(i,j,k)=hx(i,j,k)&
     &              -dt/(mu_0*dy)&
     &                 *(ez2(i,j+1,k)-ez2(i,j,k))&
     &              +dt/(mu_0*dz)&
     &                 *(ey2(i,j,k+1)-ey2(i,j,k))

             end do
          end do
```

```
        end do
!Where, mu_0 is the permeability
!of free space (in henry/meter);
! dt is the length of the time step;
! dx, dy, dz are the ditance between
!two cells in the apporpriate direction (X/Y/Z)
!In Fortran, & in an equation is considered
!to be a continuation character, which is not considered
!to be part of the statement or equation, and
!should not be mistaken as an 'operator'
!such of C language
```

If equation Eq.(2.28) and the above written code are compared then it can be noticed that the code, written above, represents the exact calcualtion of the equation to update H_x. Therefore by following this method, all the update equations for H and E, and D can be computed to simulate FDTD algorithm in Fortran.

While writing the program, it should be kept in mind that nodes at the end of the physical space do not have a neighboring nodes to one of the sides, hence leading to the problem of boundary condition (see sub-section 2.2.2). For example if the arrays are declared with 374 elements i.e. nz=ny=nx=374 (number of elements in each direction) in 3D implementation, then there is no available $E_z(375,375,375)$ for $H_x(374,374,374)$. In this situation, different boundary condition techniques should be used to update these field components.

2.5   Advantages and Limitations of FDTD Computation

According to a thesis written by Salski, 2010, [31], there are many advanatages and disadvanatges of FDTD method. But few of them are noteworhty for the objectives of this thesis. Few of those advantages and limitations of computer implementation of FDTD method are mentioned in this section.

The highlighted advantages are as follows:

1. **Easy Understanding and Visualisation of FDTD Simulation:**
   Because of Time-Domain approach of FDTD, it enables the users to visualise instantaneous propagation of electro-magnetic waves inside the scenario during

the simulation of the algorithm. This feature provides better understanding of the properties of the relative electrical device or medium, and also aids in debugging any potential problems.

2. **Better Stability and Major Error Proof:**
   FDTD algorithm is highly stable and not sensitive to computer round-off errors because of the central difference approach, which is statistically suppressed.

But along with the advantages there are also few specific limitations of FDTD computation such as:

1. When the object has very fine geometric details compared to the wavelength then it makes really difficult to achieve these details without compromising computational resources. To achieve high degree of details, the FDTD cell has to be diminished in size significantly than the size, which is restricted by the dispersion limit[4]. Therefore, time to compute this increases dramatically.

2. As mentioned earlier, FDTD algorithms require high computational resources such as memory, CPU usage, etc., in order to achieve better satisfactory simulation results.

2.6 Concluding Remarks

This chapter gives an overview idea reagrding FDTD method and the method by which it can be implemented in a computer for scientific purpose. Section 2.2 provides the important equations that are necessary for FDTD method and for the objective of this thesis. Section 2.4 shows the basics of how FDTD algorithm can be implemented in Fortran programming environment, and section 2.5 mentions the advantages and limitations of FDTD simulation in computers.

---

[4]The size limit which is set for dispersive materials

Table 2.1: Major Abbreviations Used In Chapter 2

1D	- One Dimensional
2D	- Two Dimensional
3D	- Three Dimensional
ABC	- Absorbing Boundary Condition
CPU	- Central Processing Unit
FD-FDTD	- Frequency Dependent FDTD
FDTD	- Finite Difference Time Domain method
PML	- Perfectly Matched Layer
UWB	- Ultra WideBand

Chapter 3

Computation of FDTD on GPGPU using CUDA Programming

This chapter focuses on the GPGPU parallelized computational capacity and implementation of FDTD method on GPGPU to achieve greater performance.

3.1 GPGPU - The Parallelization Monster and Computation Techniques

In Chapter 1, a brief overview of the parallelization capacity of GPU architecture was discussed (refer to Fig. 1.6). There it could be noticed that GPU's parallelized hardware capacity promoted the use of general purpose computing on GPU. For General-Purpose GPU Computing Nvidia introduced Tesla Architecture (refer to Fig. 3.2), which consist of an array of general prupose stream multi-processors. Each stream multiprocessors consist of several stream processors or processing elements. Each stream multi-rpocessor runs in Single Instruction Multiple Data[1] (SIMD) mode. This gives the complete GPGPU hardware architecture the power of two level of parallelism:

- SIMD mode of each multiprocessor providing vector style parallelism

- Multiprocessor parallelism between the processors or processing elements

---

[1] According to Flynn's Taxonomy, when a common operation is performed on multiple data points i.e. when a single instruction is computed on multiple data, it is known as SIMD mode of parallel computing

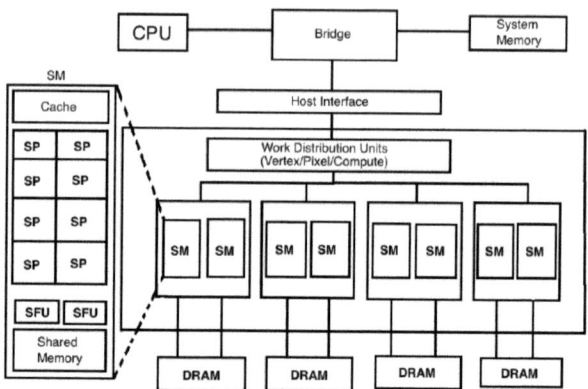

Figure 3.1: Abstract view of the Tesla unified graphics and computing GPU architecture, where SM - Streaming Multiprocessor, SP - Streaming Processor and SFU - Special Function Unit

In conjunction to parallel hardware capacity of GPGPU by Nvidia, Nvidia also introduced Compute Unified Device Architecture (CUDA) [1, 2, 15, 18, 19], which is a parallel computing platform and programming model for Nvidia's proprietory GPGPU.

On Nvidia's GPU, the computation can be accelerated (Accelerator based computing as mentioned in section 1.3) for general purpose computation in the following ways:

a) "Drop-in" Acceleration Libraries:

In this method, any application/program can be executed on a GPGPU by using Drop-in libraries [32, 33] that are tuned for GPU programming. The programmer has to apply those libraries without even having much idea about the GPU architecture, enabling acceleration of the code with minimum code changes. As mentioned in [32, 33], "Drop-in" Acceleration Libraries can be used in three steps.

Step1: Substitute normal library calls with CUDA equivalent library calls For example, instead of calling saxpy(), call cublasSaxpy() [CUDA Compatible]

Step 2: Manage Data Locality on GPU architecture For example, instead of using malloc(), memcpy(), etc., use cudaMalloc(), cudaMemcpy(), and so on.

Step 3: Rebuild and link the program / application with CUDA-accelerated libraries

b) OpenACC:

OpenACC Directive [34–36] is a programming standard developed for parallel computing platform by Portland Group (PGI), Cray, CAPS and Nvidia. OpenACC simplify and makes it easy to manage parallel programming in CPU-GPU heterogeneous system, and it supports major programming languages such as C, C++ and Fortran. These directives provide compiler hints, where the compiler automatically parallelizes that piece of code and run it on GPU (refer to snippet 3.1). As mentioned in [34–36], it can be achieved in two simple steps.

Step 1: Interpret the source code with OpenACC directives (shown in snippet 3.1)

Step 2: Compile and Run on the system with Nvidia's GPU

```
!Snippet 3.1
!Snippet of Code to show the use of OpenACC Directives

Program UpdateEquation
[Serial Code] !Serial part of the Code goes here
!$acc kernels loop !OpenACC Directive
        do k=1,nz-1
            do j=1,ny-1
                do i=2,nx-1

                    hx(i,j,k)=hx(i,j,k)&
    &                   -dt/(mu_0*dy)&
    &                       *(ez2(i,j+1,k)-ez2(i,j,k))&
    &                   +dt/(mu_0*dz)&
    &                       *(ey2(i,j,k+1)-ey2(i,j,k))

                end do
            end do
        end do
!$acc end kernels
End Program UpdateEquation
```

In the above snippet of code (3.1), it should be noticed that the OpenACC directives such as '$acc kernels loop' and '$acc end kernels' are provided after '!', which acts as a comment in fortran. OpenACC directives are mentioned as comments in fortran program because if the compiler does not support OpenACC directives then it would simply treat the code as a normal fortran program and compile it for execution on CPU. But if the compiler does support the OpenACC directives then it would compile and parallelize the selected part of the code for Nvidia's GPU computation.

c) GPGPU Programming Languages:

In this method [1, 2], programmers get maximum flexibility and power to manage and execute their code on GPU to gain maximum performance. This technique supports major programming languages such as C, C++, Fortran and their CUDA enabled languages are CUDA C, CUDA C++, CUDA Fortran, and so on. To be able to compute the program on GPGPU, the programmer just has to develop a generic parallel code and then compile and run it on the system with GPGPU. Although, implementing the generic parallel code provides power and flexibility to the programmer but to gain real performance both in case of efficiency and execution time, the programmer has to be responsible for optimizing the code for the performance (and also efficiency) and does not provide automatic parallel execution on GPU like the way OpenACC or Drop-in Libraries provide.

For the purpose of this thesis, CUDA Fotran language is chosen. The aforementioned FDTD algorithm is implemnted in CUDA Fortran in order to be able to compute on Nvidia's GPGPU.

3.2 CUDA and CUDA Fortran

With the Compute Unified Device Architecture (CUDA) and GPGPU programming languages such as CUDA Fortran, the programmer is capable of controlling the performance of the parallelized code on general purpose GPU. In order to compute the parallelized part of the computer program the programmer has to partition that part of the code into coarse grain blocks, which can be executed in parallel. These programmer specified sections, which are capable of parallel computation on GPU, are called "kernels" [1,37]. Each kernel then operates over a gird of threads. Each grid is divided into blocks in one, two or three dimensions, whereas each block is further divided into fine grain threads in one, two or three dimensions, which are capable of cooperating using shared memory and barrier synchronization. Please refer to Fig. 3.2 to get an idea reagrding the relation between kernel, grid, block and threads. Within each kernel, a thread can be identified at both block and thread level. To identify which block a thread belongs to, the CUDA defined built-in parameters such as **blockIdx%x, blockIdx%y** and **blockIdx%z**, can be used and to determine the position of the thread in the block **threadIdx%x, threadIdx%y**, and **threadIdx%z** can be used. In this way, it is easier to invoke computation across the elements in a domain or operations such as vector, matrix or volume. But it should also be kept in mind that there is a limit to the number of threads, which can be accomodated per block, because all threads of a block should reside on the same processor core and must share the limited memory resources of that core. Given the current GPU architecture, a thread block may contain upto 1024 threads. However, since a kernel can be executed by multiple thread blocks, which are equally shaped, therefore the total number of threads is equal to 'the number of threads per block' multiplied by 'the number of blocks'.

In order to execute a CUDA program on Nvidia GPUs, the programmer has to follow these steps:

- Write GPU-targeted functions i.e. kernels

- Allocate space for variables and data on the GPU

- Copy/Move data from the host (CPU) to the device (GPU), and back

- Invoke/Launch GPU subroutines/functions (kernels) from the host to run on GPU

- Use asynchronous transfers between the host (CPU) and device (GPU)

- Gather the result/output back from the GPU to the host for further analysis

- Deallocate the space for variables and data on GPU, which is allocated before

To write a kernel for a fortran program so that it can be executed on GPU, the programmer just has to keep the aforemntioned steps in mind and write the kernel in a very similar manner to the fortran programming language with certain extensions, which are mentioned in [1].

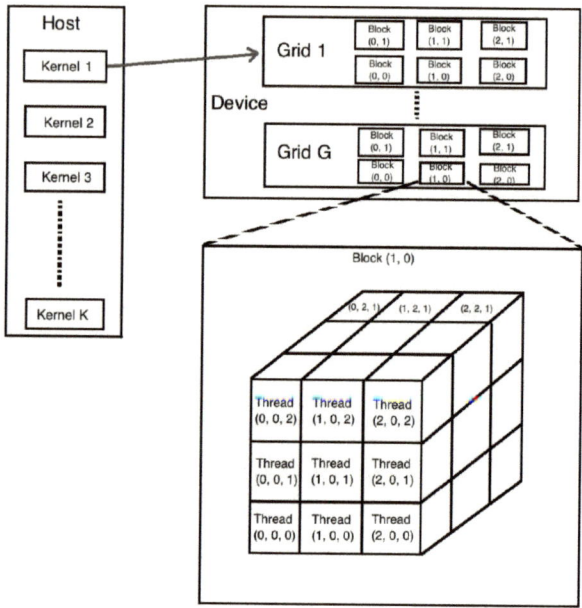

Figure 3.2: The CUDA grid organization in Tesla Architecture as mentioned in [1, 2]

3.3   CUDA Implementation of FDTD Method for GPGPU Computation

In order to compute the FDTD method on Nvidia GPU, the points regarding CUDA implementation, which are discussed in previous section (3.2), should be taken into consideration. Therefore, if the example of update equation of H_x is taken into consideration then the first step is to invoke the GPU kernel from the host code and in order to do that the code to invoke the kernel should look like the following:

```
call update_hx_r <<< dimGrid,dimBlock >>> &
&          (nx,ny,nz, ay,az, d_hx,d_ey2,d_ez2)


!where, dimGrid = dim3(ny,nz,1) &
!dimBlock = dim3(nx,1,1) for this project.
!And d_hx,d_ey2,d_ez2 are equivalent to variables hx, ey2, ez2,
!but specific for the device (GPU).
```

In the above snippet of code, **dim3** is a type of integer vector, which is based on uint3 and is used to specify dimensions. If any component is left unspecified while defining type dim3 then it is simply initialized to 1. **dimGrid** specifies the dimensions of the grid and is of type dim3. Whereas, **dimBlock** specifies the dimensions of the block and is also of type dim3. It should always be kept in mind that dimGrid and dimBlock should be defined based on the program specifications and implementation of the programmer.

Now, since the kernel to be invoked is specified, it is time to write the CUDA equivalent of the update equtation of H_x, as follows:

```
!CUDA Fortran code for Update Equation of Hx
attributes(global) subroutine
                update_hx(nx,ny,nz, ay,az, hx,ey2,ez2)

    implicit none

    integer, value :: nx,ny,nz
    real, value :: ay,az

    REAL,device :: hx(1:nx,1:ny,1:nz),ey2(1:nx,1:ny,1:nz)
```

```
REAL,device :: ez2(1:nx,1:ny,1:nz)

REAL :: r_hx

integer :: i,j,k

i = threadidx%x
j = blockidx%x
k = blockidx%y


if ((i.ge.2).and.(i.le.nx-1).and.(j.ge.1).and.&
&(j.le.ny-1).and.(k.ge.1).and.(k.le.nz-1)) then

            r_hx =hx(i,j,k) &
    &           - ay * (ez2(i,j+1,k)-ez2(i,j,k)) &
    &           + az * (ey2(i,j,k+1)-ey2(i,j,k))

            hx(i,j,k) = r_hx

endif

   return
end subroutine update_hx
```

It should be noticed from the above snippet of code that to implement the update equation as CUDA kernel, the triple for-loops (for i, j, k) of the general update equation are simply eliminated and replaced as the core functionality into the kernel, which is implemented in the way as shown in the snippet. Therefore, by following the above implementation of CUDA kernel for all field updates, boundary conditions, convergence checks, and data input/output (I/O), the FDTD method can be implemented on Nvidia GPU and computed to achieve better performance by taking advantage of high parallelism of GPUs.

3.4 Computation on Nvidia's General Purpose GPU

There are many ways in which FDTD can be implemented on GPU hardware, which are mentioned properly in [37–40]. Since actual implementation approaches of FDTD method on GPU hardware would vary based on the programmer and/or the application of FDTD method itself and is not within the scope of this thesis, therefore, the actualy implementation method is not discussed in details in this thesis. But to understand the problem, which is the focus of this thesis, it is worth knowing the insights of the computation on GPU hardware.

3.4.1 GPU Hardware and support for FDTD Computation

As mentioned in an article by Wolfe [41], a GPU is designed for stream or throughput computing and it does not support a deep cache memory hierarchy[2] for memory performance like the one which is common in CPU computing. Nvidia GPU has a number of stream multiprocessors, which executes concurrently with others. Each multiprocessor contains groups of stream processors. A kepler stream multiprocessor generally consist of 12 groups of 16 stream processors. Each stream processor is capable of executing a sequential thread in a way, which is called as Single Instruction, Multiple Thread (SIMT) by Nvidia. All stream processors in the same group are capable of executing the same instruction at the same time, which is similar to the execution of SIMD mode. Since, algorithms such as FDTD performs small amounts of calculations on large amounts of data, which is very similar to SIMD computation, therefore FDTD acts as a perfect candidate for computation on GPU.

On Nvidia GPU, the codes are executed in group of 32 threads, which are called 'warps'. Each thread in the warp are capable of executing in parallel as long as they are executing the same instruction on different pieces of data. Since FDTD computation requires similar calculations on large amount of data, hence, memory bandwidth plays an important role in the performance of FDTD computation. Nvidia GPU supports small software-managed data cache, which is attached to each stream multiprocessor and are shared among the stream processors. The software-managed data cache on each multiprocessor is a low-latency, high-bandwidth, indexable memory, who's operating speed is almost similar to register's operating speed. Since a GPU is meant for stream or throughput computing, hence having physical cache memories are ineffective

---

[2]Having various level of cache memory hierarchy such as L1, L2, etc., in order to compensate the latency gap between the main memory and the CPU

for computational purposes. But because of the latency gap between the main memory and the GPU, to compensate with this gap, GPU uses a high degree of multithreading i.e. issue multiple threads for computation at the same time. Whenever a thread has to fetch a memory, which usually takes around hundred clock cycles for GPU, the GPU either spawns new threads for computational purposes or switch context between the threads. GPU threads can switch contexts nearly instantaneously and this enables the GPU to conpensate memory latency by launching high multitude (in hundreds to thousands) of threads simultaneously and performing rapid context switching while the threads wait for input data.

CUDA enabled GPUs offer several types of memory, of which three are very important with respect to FDTD computation: **shared, constant and device (GPU) memory**. Shared memory is cached on GPU multiprocessor with very low latency and can be accessed by the group of threads. Constant memory is cached as read-only section of the memory and is limited in space. On current GPUs there are dedicated memories for computation pruposes and are called device memories. The device memory is a high latency memory as well, but has lower latency gap than the one for main system memory and GPU. GPU kernels execute with an implicit barrier synchronization. Since, multiprocessors execute asynchronously in parallel, hence it is not feasible to share data among threads of different multiprocessors using conventional parallel computing tcchninques. For that reason, the programmer has to aproach a different method in order to perform that. When threads in single block are executed on the same multiprocessor, they can synchronize and share data with threads in the same block using the software data cache of the multiprocessor.

If FDTD method is taken into consideration then it can be noticed that according to Yee Cell, the field components (magnetic and electric) are arranged in a staggered manner, which allows their computation to be staggered in time by half a time step. Therefore, when electric fields are computed using the values of four surrounding magnetic fields, the magnetic fields are treated as constants, and the process is reversed when the magnetic fields are computed. This concept of FDTD computation aids in rapid context switching of threads on GPU and therefore the performance of FDTD computation on GPU are phenomenal.

Now, according to [41], performance of computation on NVIDIA GPUs requires optimizing of the following architectural features:

- Exploring enough parallelism to populate all the multiprocessors

- Using enough additional parallelism to allow multithreading to keep the stream processors busy

- Optimizing device memory accesses for contiguous/non-contiguos data to compensate the latency gap between memory and device (GPU)

- Utilizing the software data cache to store intermediate results, which may be useful for future computational purposes

While computing FDTD on GPU, the first two requirements crtiteria of eploring parallelism and populating multiprocessors with enough task to keep them busy, are easy to deal with. But when it comes to optimizing device memory access and utilizing shared data cache to improve the performance of FDTD method even more, then it becomes really difficult to deal with these issues. Computing architecture on each stream multiprocessor of GPU can be visualised as Split Shared Memory Parallel Computer Architecture, which is mentioned in Chapter1 (section 1.2.1), and to improve the performance of computation in such an architecture it is very important to optimize the memory accesses.

3.4.2 Memory Coalescing

The performance of computation is not just affected by the number of memory accesses, but the performance is also dependant on how the memory is being accessed. In GPU hardware, there are two types of memory accesses in general: Coalesced memory access (Memory Coalescing) and Uncoalesced memory access (Non-sequential Access/Unaligned Memory Access).

Coalesced memory access on GPU is referred to the method of combining multiple memory accesses into a single transaction[3]. Coalesce memory accesses is used to minimize the number of bus transactions in order to increase performance. In best practices, one memory transaction will be issued for a half-warp (16 threads). Although memory can be accessed by a full-warp (32 consecutive threads) in a single transaction, but there is a high possbility that it might result into Uncoalesced load, i.e., memory access becomes serialized, if the following are affirmative [42,43]:

- Memory is not sequential

- Memory access is sparse

---

[3]One memory-transaction is referred to process of executing load and store instruction in an atomic way

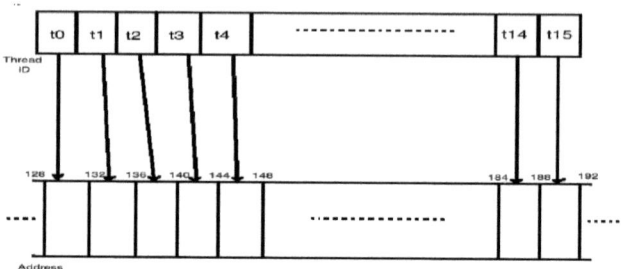

Figure 3.3: All threads of half-warp participate

- Misaligned/Unaligned memory access

Coalesced memory access using Aligned Access: A coordinated read is performed by a half-warp (16 threads) to a contiguous region of global (device) memory. This can be achieved in two ways: One where all threads participate (Fig. 3.3) and another way where some threads do not particiapte[4] (Fig. 3.4). The contiguous region of global memory may vary in size depending on the type of data being accessed by the threads. The size can be of 64, 128 and 256 bytes. For 64 bytes, each thread reads a word of type int, float. For 128 bytes, each thread reads a double-word of type long, double. For 256 bytes, each thread reads a quad-word of type int4, float4. But for coalesced memory access it should be kept in mind that:

- Starting address for accessing must be a multiple of region size

- The 'n'th thread in a half-warp (16 threads) must access the 'n'th element in a block, which is being read

Uncoalesced memory access: When the memory access is sequential but unaligned (Fig. 3.5) or when the memory is permuted accessed by threads (Fig. 3.6) resulting in aligned but non-sequential access then it can be called as Uncoalesced memory access. Because of uncoalesced memory access, it requires more than one transaction to load the words. However, it should be kept in mind that even if the memory access is aligned but not sequnetial, it is possible to combine the access pattern into a single

---

[4]This may occur due to divergence within a half-warp (16 threads)

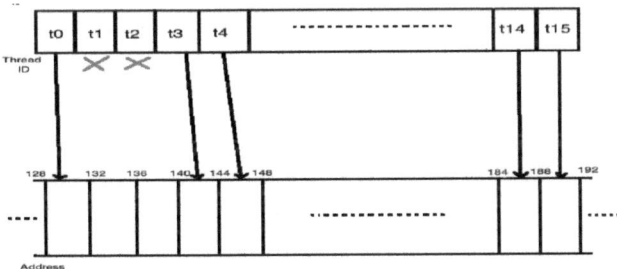

Figure 3.4: Some Threads Do Not Participate

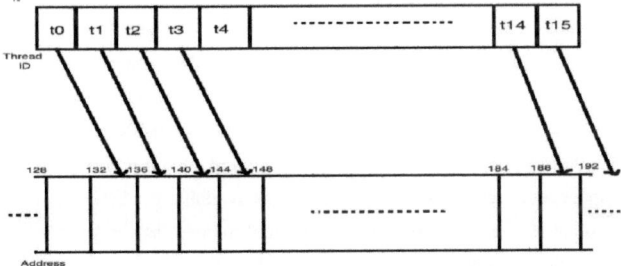

Figure 3.5: Unaligned Starting Address which is not a multiple of region size i.e. 64 for this case

transaction, which may then lead to coalesced memory access, but this technique will require advanced programming envisions.

3.5 Execution of FDTD Method on GPU Hardware

In section 3.3, the implemntation of GPU kernel to compute FDTD method on GPU was explored, but in order to get a better idea regarding how to execute the kernels on GPU in order to achieve better efficiency and performance, it is necessary to understand the methodology behind execution of each thread of the kernel. For computational purposes, the FDTD method can be implemented in such as way that each

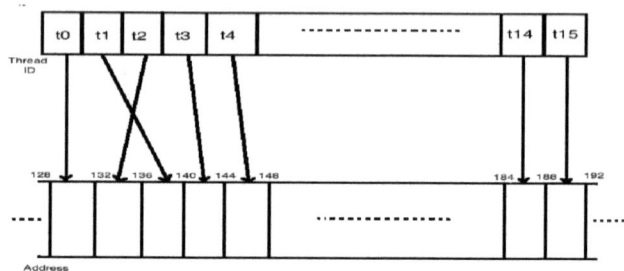

Figure 3.6: Permuted Access by Threads

thread[5] within each block is allocated to at least one cell in the FDTD space, hence, exposing the maximum available parallelism in the algorithm. When a GPU kernel is invoked to launch, two *dim3* type variables are mentioned: one to represent the organization of blocks within a grid and another one to represent the organization of threads within each block. Each thread either computes on one or more cells in the FDTD space, depending on the ratio of threads available per block to N_x. If the threads are executed on a series of cells in sequntial manner, as shown in Fig. 3.7, then the approach is uncoalesced memory access. But if the threads are executed on each cells in an interleaved manner then the threads simultaneously request adjacent memory locations, completing in one memory transaction, and therefore this apporach is coalesced memory access. Refer to Fig. 3.8 to see the coalesced memory access implementation of FDTD method. A detailed implementation guide is provided in a paper by M. Livesey [37]. Depending on these two memory access approaches of FDTD method, many techniques can be implemnted to compensate the latency gap between the main memory and the device (GPU).

---

[5]Whether all these threads are executed in parallel or not will depend on the available streaming multiprocessors on the GPU hardware

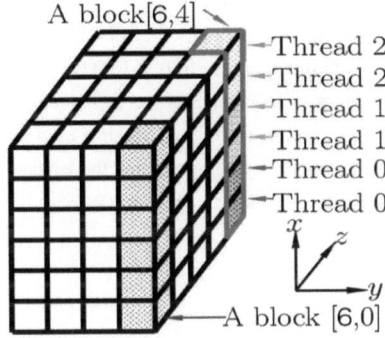

Figure 3.7: Uncoalesced memory access for multiple threads (three in this case) in a block [6, b], where [a, b] means [blockIdx%x, blockIdx%y]

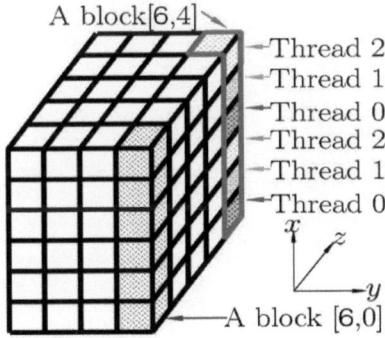

Figure 3.8: Coalesced memory access for multiple threads (three in this case) in a block [6, b], where [a, b] means [blockIdx%x, blockIdx%y]

3.6 Concluding Remarks

In this chapter, the hadrware and software techniques of CUDA and Nvidia GPU are discussed along with the computation of FDTD method on GPU. To improve the efficiency of the data input/output (I/O) of FDTD computation on GPU, the CUDA architecture and the parallel computational techniques used on GPU should be kept in mind. The main technique (solution), which is used in this thesis in order to improve the efficiency of data I/O by compensating the latency gap between the memory and the GPU, is mentioned in the next chapter (Chap. 4).

Table 3.1: Major Abbreviations Used In Chapter 3

CUDA	- Compute Unified Device Architecture
FDTD	- Finite Difference Time Domain method
GPU	- General Purpose Graphics Processing Unit
GPGPU	- Graphics Processing Unit
SIMD	- Single Instruction Multiple Data
SIMT	- Single Instruction, Multiple Thread

Chapter 4

The Solution to The Problem

4.1 The Problem - Revisited

As the problem mentioned in section 1.3, it was noticed that performance of computation on the GPU is dependant on the memory transfer between the CPU (host) & GPU (device), and the latency gap between the main memory and the device plays a key role in that computational performance. Again, in section 3.4, it was noticed that during FDTD computation on GPU, memory can be accessed either from shared, constant and device (GPU) memory. By using coalesced memory access the performance of FDTD computation can be improved more on GPU, which is mentioned properly in a paper by M. Livesey [37]. Therefore, to sumarize overall performance of FDTD computation is depdendant on two types of memory accesses: one between host & device, and the other one in the GPU itself, based on different types of memory in GPU. Refer to Fig. 4.1 to get an idea regarding the memory access.

Since, many different methods to increase the performance of FDTD computation in GPU by managing memory accesses inside the GPU, have already been proposed and implemented. The main purpose of this thesis is to increase the performance of data input/output (I/O) of FDTD computation by increasing the efficiency of memory management of data I/O between the device and the host. The novel solution to this issue is proposed in the next section.

4.2 The Solution

The novel approach which is proposed in this thesis actually tries to optimize the memory access from the GPU to the main memory. This is achieved by introducing the

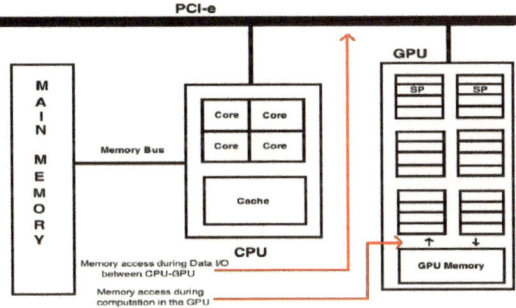

Figure 4.1: Different types of memory access required for FDTD Computation on GPU

concept of **'Buffer'** in the FDTD computation.

In computing, **Data Buffer** [44] can be implemented as a region on the physical memory storage used to temporarily store data, which may be moved from one place to another. In the world of High Performance Computing, when processes have on work on a piece of data, which has to be moved from one process to another, the technique to use data buffer is often used. The technique of data buffer is used while sending data from the sender to the receiver in order to hold the data being transferred. Buffers are very popular in implementation in input/output (I/O) of hardware devices and uses the First in, First out (FIFO)[1] method to output the data. Another technique, which is also very popular in data transfer and holding the data for future usage, is called **'Cache'**. But the basic difference between a buffer and a cache is that cache holds data, which has high possibility to be accessed again in near future, whereas, buffer only holds the data temporarily while the data is being transferred or communicated.

Since, the FDTD computation on General Purpose GPU can be imagined as a continuos sender-receiver computation, therefore this simple solution of introducing buffer for the data input/output (I/O) of FDTD computation improves the performance and optimizes the memory access by compensating the lantency gap between the memory-host-GPU. When a program is computed on the CPU (host) and then the GPU kernel is launched to be able to compute on the GPU, then a CPU can be thought as a sender and the GPU can be thought as a receiver. In the same way, when the GPU completes the computation and sends back the computed data (output) to the CPU for further

---

[1]FIFO: Data which comes first, is shown/transferred as an outout first

analysis or some other operation to be done by the CPU, then the GPU can be thought of as a sender and the CPU as a receiver.

In the FDTD implemtation of this thesis, when the FDTD method is computed on GPU, after each kernel is executed, the update equations of H or E produces the output, which is needed by other kernels in order to calculate the E or H of the next time step. In general, during this brief time of multiple kernel execution, the intermediate output data, which is used to calculate the update equations of next time step, is transferred to the CPU from the GPU, and this incurs a big latency gap resulting into performance degradation. But by using the buffer technique, this latency gap can be optimized. When the intermediate data output is genearted by the update equations of previous time-step, instead of copying the data to the CPU or the main memory, the data is hold onto a data buffer[2], which is implemented in the program. Therefore, when the GPU tries to fetch the output as the input for the update equations of next time-step, instead of fetching the data from the memory, it fetches the data from the software-implemented buffer on the GPU itself, avoiding the high-latency memory access. Fig. 4.2 shows the diagramatic representation of software-implemented buffer. Fig. 4.2.(A) shows the transfer of data output from GPU to CPU without buffer. Fig. 4.2.(B) and Fig. 4.2.(C) show the diagramatic representation of the implementation of software-implemented buffer.

4.3 Programmatic Implementation of the Solution

The GPU hardware already has software-implemented cache on each multiprocessor, which is shared by the threads of that multiprocessors. In section 3.4, it was already reviewed that how coalesced and un-coalesced memory access with the combintation of shared memory (cache) affect the performance of computation on GPU. It should be noted that cache memories are good hold data, which have more probability of being accessed quite often in future for computational purpose. But for FDTD computation, the data output or input value are only nedded for next or previous time-step (1 time-step) only. Therefore, using programmatic caching technique to hold the temporary data I/O would be expensive in terms of resources and cost-efficiency. Instead, a programmatic approach to implement data buffer is much more suitable for the purpose.

---

[2]Can be thought of software-implemented data buffer

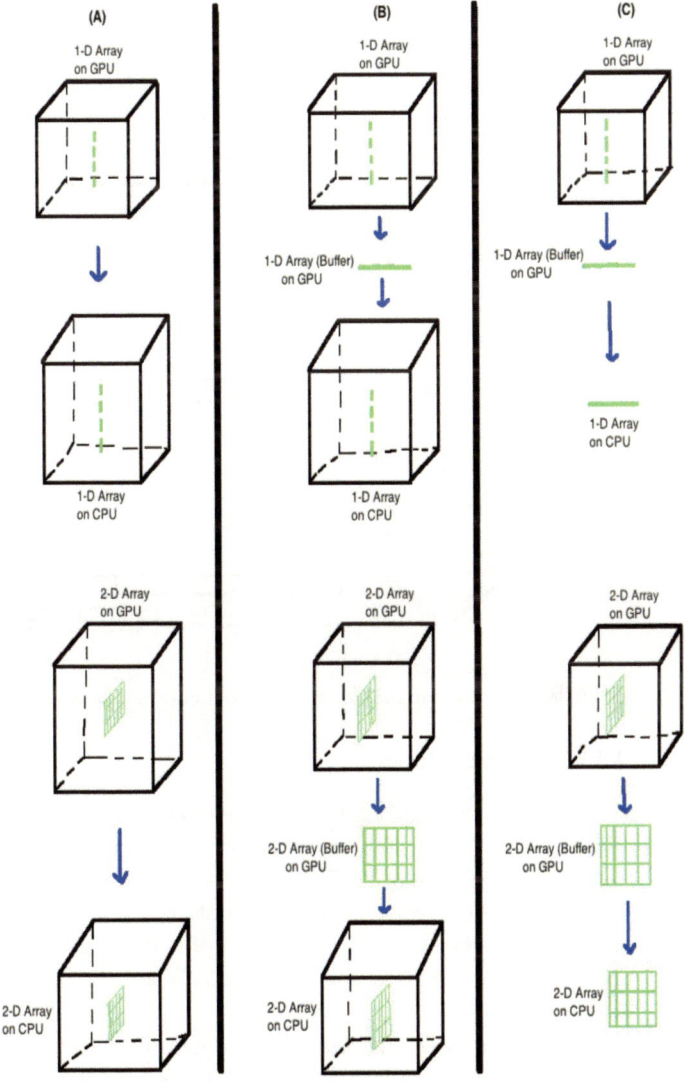

Figure 4.2: Three (A, B, C) Methods of Data-Output. Method B and C implements buffer to fetch output data to the CPU

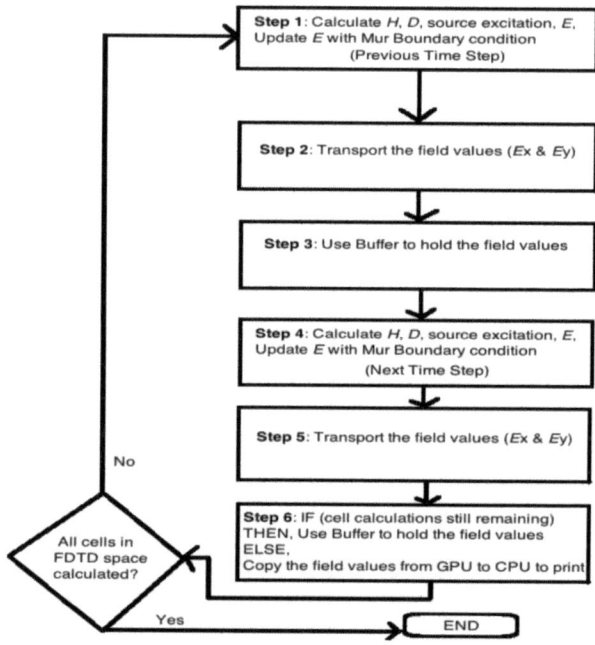

Figure 4.3: Flowchart to show the use of Buffer in FDTD computation on GPU

4.3.1 Implementation

Fig. 4.3 shows how to implement programmatic data buffer in FDTD computation on GPU in the form of flowchart. From the figure, it can be noticed that in step 2 (or in step 6) when the field values of E are transported so that they can be used to update H, it is useful to use buffer in this place. If the buffer is not implemented in this place then the field values will be copied back to the CPU and the GPU has to fetch the values again from the CPU for further computation, which will result into performance degradation.

In order to implement the data buffer, a seperate GPU kernel is written for this purpose. The implementation of buffer as GPU kerenl is as follows:

```
!Snippet 4.1
!Implementation of Data buffer for 2-D plane-XY
```

```
!where X is represented by i and
!Y is represented by j

attributes(global) subroutine set_buffer_2d_xy &
& (nx,ny,nz, d_output_3D, d_output_2d_xy, src_k)

!Where d_output_3D is the data output in array format, which is
!to be stored on the buffer and
!d_output_2d_xy is the buffer array that holds the values
!src_i, src_j, src_k are the source points for
!i, j, k respectively

  implicit none

  integer, value :: nx,ny,nz
  integer, value :: src_k
  REAL,device :: d_output_3D(1:nx,1:ny,1:nz)
  REAL,device :: d_output_2d_xy(1:nx,1:ny)

  integer :: i,j,k

  k = src_k

  i = threadidx%x
  j = blockidx%x

if ((i.ge.1).and.(i.le.nx).and.(j.ge.1).and.(j.le.ny)) then

  d_output_2d_xy(i,j) = d_output_3D(i,j,k) !Buffer

endif

  return

end subroutine set_buffer_2d_xy
```

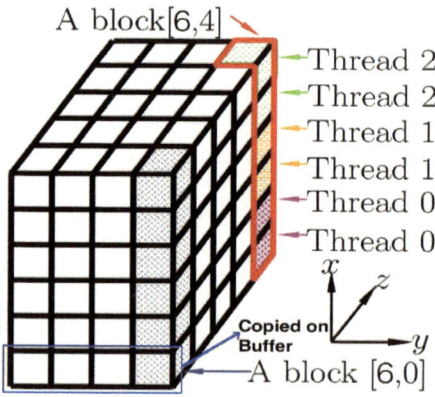

Figure 4.4: Visual representation of data copied on Buffer based on code snippet 4.1: 2-D Buffer Implementation with un-coalesced memory access approach of FDTD computation on GPU

From the code snippet it can be noticed that this buffer is implemnted for 2-D array (XY) i.e. a plane of XY, which represents FDTD cells on one face of the grid. i and j represent the position of each cell on the plane. Fig. 4.4 shows how the above code snippet uses the buffer technique to hold field values temporarily in un-coalesced memory access implemntation of FDTD method. Although the buffer technique can be implemnted for both coalesced and un-coalesced memory access apporach, where coalesced memory access along with programmatic-implementation of buffer should result into better performance theoretically.

It should be kept in mind that the implemntation of buffer mentioned in snippet 4.1 is only for excitation location for one configuration (for XY). The implemntation will vary for different configuration of different excitation location such as 2-D XZ, 2-D YZ, 1-D X, 1-D Y, 1-D Z, etc (refer to Fig. 4.5). To implement the buffer in different configuration, only i, j and k need to be assigned different values accordingly.

Different values of i, j and k based on different configuration are as follows:

```
!Snippet 4.2

!Where src_i, src_j, src_k are the source points for
!i, j, k respectively
```

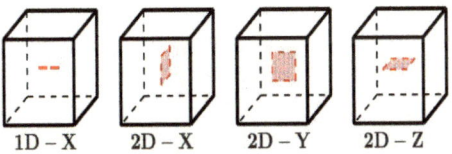

Figure 4.5: Excitation location at different axis and dimensions

```
!i, j, k values for Buffer Configuration for 2-D XZ
  j = src_j
  i = threadidx%x
  k = blockidx%x


!i, j, k values for Buffer Configuration for 2-D YZ
  i = src_i
  j = threadidx%x
  k = blockidx%x


!i, j, k values for Buffer Configuration for 1-D X
  i = threadidx%x + (blockidx%x * 512)
  j = src_j
  k = src_k


!i, j, k values for Buffer Configuration for 1-D Y
  i = src_i
  j = threadidx%x + (blockidx%x * 512)
  k = src_k


!i, j, k values for Buffer Configuration for 1-D Z
  i = src_i
  j = src_j
  k = threadidx%x + (blockidx%x * 512)


!blockDim = 512 for this FDTD computation
```

```
!i.e. i,j,k values in each block will range
!from 0-511 (512 values) and each thread has an unique
!threadidx value defined by
!threadidx%x + blockidx%x * blockDim%x
!Each thread block can have to upto 1024 threads
!in CUDA 3.0 and later
```

While implementing the buffer for 1-D array, the loop to iterate in order to store all the values of data I/O in a 1-D array should be either for i or j or k depending on the axis. For example to store the data I/O in the buffer for configuration of 1-D X the ietration should be:

```
if ((i.ge.1).and.(i.le.nx)) then

    d_output_x(i) = d_output_3D(i,j,k)

endif
```

Therefore, it can be noticed that for X axis the iteration is from cell 1 to N_x and only i is used. For Y and Z, cells of N_y and N_z should be iterated through j and k respectively.

Implementation for Random Points: To implement the buffer technique to hold data input/output on random excitation points, the implementation is very similar except the values of the points (cells) through which X, Y, Z i.e. i, j, k, will be iterated for programming purpose, will vary. Even the invocation of the kernel for the buffer will vary, which is mentioned in the next subsection.

4.3.2 Invoking Buffer Kernel

Once the GPU kernel for buffer technique is implemented in the program, it is now important to invoke/launch the kernel at appropriate duration of computation as mentioned in Fig. 4.3. One example of invocation is as follows:

```
!lanuch the kernel for buffer
      call set_buffer_2d_xy &
&         <<< dim3(ny,1,1), dim3(nx,1,1) >>> &
&           (nx,ny,nz, d_ex,d_output_2d_xy, src(0,2))
!Where d_ex is the computed value of Ex on the device (GPU)
```

```
!copy the data from GPU to CPU
     h_output_2d_xy(1:nx,1:ny) = d_output_2d_xy(1:nx,1:ny)
```

After calculating the field values, source excitation, boundary condition in each time-step, the above mentioned kernel for buffer technique should be invoked, so that before the field values are copied back to the CPU from the GPU, the buffer arrays on the GPU should hold the field values, which are necessary for future computation of FDTD. In this way the GPU do not have to access the main memory every time for data input for next time-step because the necessary field values are already existing on the buffer in the GPU. It should be noted that the above code only shows the example of invoking the buffer to store the data output for E_x, but the kernel should be invoked for to store all the data output values for E, H and D for X, Y and Z directions. In order to use buffer technique at random points, it is essential for the programmer to invoke the kernel where it is necessary.

4.4 Possible Limitations and their Solutions

When data buffers are implemented on hardware, the two most common limitations that are faced are as follows:

Buffer Overflow & its solution: This phenomenon occurs when the buffer receives more data than it can hold. This issue arrises becuase the size of the buffer on the hardware is fixed. Therefore, some of the data can not be accomodated on the buffer if the size of data is more than the size of the buffer. To handle this issue, the implementation of the GPU kernel for the software-implemented buffer is approached in a different way. In the implementation it can be noticed that the size of the buffer array is dynamic in nature and is of the size of the data, which is being stored on the buffer.

Buffer Under-run & its solution: This is another common issue with hardware implemented buffer technique. On the hardware, the buffers have limited bandwidth for data transfer. If the data, which is being stored, is received at a low bandwidth, this reduces the performance of the communication between the two devices, which are using that buffer. For the buffer implemntation in this thesis, this issue is not a challenge because the buffer technique mentioned here is software-implemented (programmed) and therefore, the speed of the data stored on the buffer is as per the computation speed of the program itself. Another point to be remembered that the buffer technique mentioned in this thesis is not used to communicate between two devices but to hold data, which are required for future computational purposes.

Therefore, the two most common issues with buffer implemntation are solved for the methodology implemented in this thesis.

4.5 Concluding Remarks

Although a novel solution of using buffer to optimize the memory access problem for data input/output (I/O) of FDTD method is porposed, but the success of the implemntation of this solution is yet to be reviewed through testing and validation process, which is discussed in the next chapter.

Table 4.1: Major Abbreviations Used In Chapter 3

CPU	- Central Processing Unit
FDTD	- Finite Difference Time Domain method
FIFI	- First in, First out
GPU	- General Purpose Graphics Processing Unit
GPGPU	- Graphics Processing Unit

Chapter 5

Evaluation and Validation of The Solution

In this Chapter, the effectiveness of the implemnted solution is discussed along with the critical analysis of the performance of the method used.

5.1 Testing of the Implemented Solution

The implemented solution of using buffers to compensate the latency gap between the main memory and the GPU, is tested on various environment in order to review the success rate of the implementation. The environments used for the testing prupose and the test results are provided as follows.

5.1.1 Input Parameters for FDTD Computation

For testing purposes, two types of input parameters for FDTD computation were chosen, which are as follows:

Test Parameter 1:

```
nx_ny_nz: 374 374 374
t_max (No. of Time-steps): 30
source_type:  soft
elements_per_wavelength: 100
wave_frequency: 3.0D9 (3.0000000E+09)
pulse_width: 0.5
```

```
pulse_modulation_frequency: 0
number_of_excitation_sources: 10000
source_location_start: 187 101 101
source_location_end:    187 200 200
!various input values for the frquency of the pulse/wave are provid
pulse_type: 2
fsigma (sigma): 0
feps_s (epsilon): 1
feps_inf: 1
ftau_d (tau): 0
feps_m: 1.0
ftau_2: 0 .0
alpha: 0.1
```

In test parameter 1, the mesh size is 374*374*374 i.e. 52313624, or 52.313624 million mesh cells are computed on for 30 time-steps using the various variable values as mentioned above.

Test Parameter 2:

```
nx_ny_nz: 250 250 250
t_max (No. of Time-steps): 30
source_type:   soft
elements_per_wavelength: 100
wave_frequency: 3.0D9 (3.0000000E+09)
pulse_width: 0.5
pulse_modulation_frequency: 0
number_of_excitation_sources: 10000
source_location_start: 187 101 101
source_location_end:    187 200 200
!various input values for the frquency of
!the pulse/wave are provided
pulse_type: 2
fsigma (sigma): 0
feps_s (epsilon): 1
feps_inf: 1
ftau_d (tau): 0
```

```
feps_m: 1.0
ftau_2: 0 .0
alpha: 0.1
```

In test parameter 2, the mesh size is 250*250*250 i.e. 15625000, or 15.625 million mesh cells are computed on for 30 time-steps using the various variable values as mentioned above. In test parameter 2, only the number of mesh cells is changed in order to get a good evaluation on whether the implemented solution is effective or not.

5.1.2 Hardware Environment

To execute the FDTD program, the following system with GPU of Kepler architecture was used.

Computational System Environment

```
System: Fujitsu PRIMERGY CX400
CPU name: 43 Xeon E5-2680
CPU microarchitecture: Sandy-Bridge
CPU clock(GHz): 2.7
CPUs(cores)/node: 2 (8)
host memory/node(GB): 128
Level 1 cache in CPU(KB): 32 X 2
Level 2 cache in CPU(KB): 256 X 2
Level 3 cache in CPU(MB): 20
Peak performance in single precision (GFLOPS) on CPU: 172.8
Peak performance in double precision (GFLOPS) on CPU: 86.4
GPU name: Tesla K20Xm
No. of GPU used: 1
Number of streaming multiprocessors: 14
Number of SP cores per SM: 192
L2 level cache size per SP (KB): 1536
Maximum threads per block: 1024
GPU clock (MHz): 732
Clock speed per streaming core (MHz) processor: 735
Type of global memory: GDDR5
Global memory size(GB): 6
```

```
Bus width(bit): 384
Global memory bandwidth (GB/s): 250
Peak performance of GPGPU
in single precision(GFLOPS): 3950
Peak performance of GPGPU
in double precision(GFLOPS): 1310
```

5.1.3 Test Results

For the first few tests (Test 1-4), to check whether the buffer technique is providing any speedup to the existing FDTD computation on GPU, the FDTD program was executed with and without buffer implementation with test parameters 1 & 2 on the computational systems envrionment, which are mentioned above. For the tests the excitation was chosen on 2-D plane of XY. One thing to be noticed is that the 'time' in the results is the total execution time of the program on the GPU and the 'speed' is the total execution time divided by the number of time steps. These two variabes are of most importance for the critical analysis purpose.

The test results were noted as follows:

Test 1 Result

```
!Test Results
!For 374 * 374 *374 mesh cells for 30 time-steps
!Without Buffer Implementation

nx_ny_nz:      374            374            374
 t_max:              30
 elements_per_wavelength:            100
 wave_frequency:     3.0000000E+09
 pulse_width:     0.5000000
 pulse_modulation_frequency:      0.000000
 number_of_excitation_sources:          10000
 source location:   187         101            101
 pulse_type:      2
 fsigma:      0.000000
 feps_s:      1.000000
```

```
feps_i:     1.000000
ftau_d:     0.000000

timeskip:    1.000000
dt:    1.9245009E-12

dx:     1.0000000E-03
dy:     1.0000000E-03
dz:     1.0000000E-03

mu_0:    1.2566371E-06
eps_0:    8.8419411E-12

          30   time steps

count:    4.3610243E+08
time:     446.3610        s
speed:     14.87870       s/timistep
```

Test 2 Result

```
!Test Results
!For 374 * 374 *374 mesh cells for 30 time-steps
!With Buffer Implementation

nx_ny_nz:              374           374           374
t_max:              30
elements_per_wavelength:            100
wave_frequency:    3.0000000E+09
pulse_width:     0.5000000
pulse_modulation_frequency:     0.000000
number_of_excitation_sources:          10000
source location:            187          101          101
pulse_type:           2
fsigma:     0.000000
feps_s:     1.000000
```

```
feps_i:      1.000000
ftau_d:      0.000000

timeskip:    1.000000
dt:     1.9245009E-12

dx:     1.0000000E-03
dy:     1.0000000E-03
dz:     1.0000000E-03

mu_0:      1.2566371E-06
eps_0:     8.8419411E-12

          30  time steps

count:      4.0787398E+08
time:       407.8740      s
speed:      13.59580      s/timistep
```

Test Result 3

```
!Test Results
!For 250 * 250 * 250 mesh cells for 30 time-steps
!Without Buffer Implementation

nx_ny_nz:              250          250          250
 t_max:                30
 timeskip:    1.000000
          30  time steps

 count:      4.1489243E+08
 time:       414.8920      s
 speed:      13.82970      s/timistep
```

Test 4 Result

```
!Test Results
```

```
!For 250 * 250 * 250 mesh cells for 30 time-steps
!With Buffer Implementation

nx_ny_nz:               250          250          250
 t_max:                  30
 timeskip:        1.000000
                30  time steps


 count:        4.0203915E+08
 time:         402.0390      s
 speed:         13.40130      s/timistep
```

Tests 1 - 4 verifies whether the buffer implementation is working properly. It should be noted that for Test 3 and 4, the parts of the test results, which are common such as variables used for the wave/pulse, are omitted because of redundancy in all test results.

Test 5 shows the result of implementing buffer technique for random excitation point on the FDTD mesh.

Test 5 Result

```
!Test Results
!For 374 * 374 *374 mesh cells for 30 time-steps
!With Buffer Implementation on Random excitation points

nx_ny_nz:               374          374          374
 t_max:                  30
 timeskip:        1.000000
                30  time steps


 count:        4.0788150E+08
 time:         407.8815      s
 speed:         13.59605      s/timistep
```

5.2 Critical Analysis & Evaluation of Test Results

5.2.1 Speed-Up Analysis

In order to analyse and evaluate the performance of the implemented buffer technique, the speedup of the execution with respect to time was evaluated for the test results. It should be kept in mind that for all the tests (1-5) the number of processors or processing-nodes utilized were same and therefore, the speedup in execution is not evaluated based on the number of processing nodes used but by analysing the speedup in execution time due to change in parallelising approach in the program.

In general, the formula to calculate speedup using execution time for same number of processing nodes is given by:

$$S = \frac{T_s}{T_p} \qquad (5.1)$$

where, T_s is the time taken for execution of sequential algorithm and T_s is the time taken for execution of parallel algorithm with 'p' processors/processing nodes.

But for this thesis, since the implementation of FDTD method is already parallelised and the number of processing nodes are same for all the tests performed, therefore, the speedup formula can be represented as:

$$S = \frac{T_{old}}{T_{new}} \qquad (5.2)$$

where, T_{old} is the time taken for execution of the old program and T_{new} is the time taken for execution of the new program.

For test 1 and test 2 (refer to Fig. 5.1), where the total execution time is 446.3610 and 407.8740 seconds (refer to the test results provided in previous pages) respectively, the evaluation was performed and the speedup was found to be:

$$\begin{aligned} S = \frac{T_{old}}{T_{new}} &= \frac{446.3610}{407.8740} \\ &= 1.0943600229 \end{aligned} \qquad (5.3)$$

Therefore, the speedup gained by implementing the buffer is 1.09x (times) approximately (refer to Fig. 5.2).

For test 3 and test 4, where the total execution time is 414.8920 and 402.0390 seconds (refer to the test results provided in previous pages) respectively, the evaluation

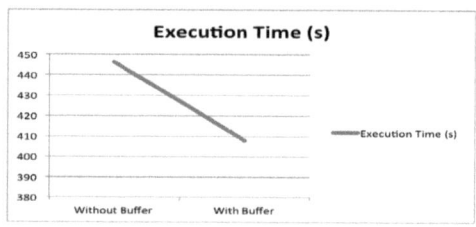

Figure 5.1: Execution Time for Test 1 & 2 in seconds. *Less is better in performance*

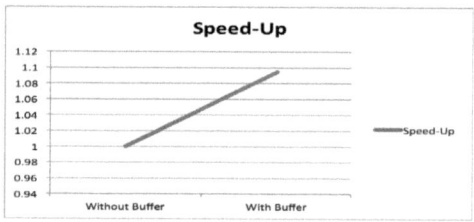

Figure 5.2: Speedup result of Test 1 & 2. *More is better*

was performed and the speedup was found to be:

$$S = \frac{T_{old}}{T_{new}} = \frac{414.8920}{402.0390}$$
$$= 1.0319695353$$

(5.4)

Therefore, the speedup gained by implementing the buffer is 1.03x (times) approximately (refer to Fig. 5.3).

Many other tests were performed (by changing configuration of the planes) in order to analyse the behaviour and performance of the implemented buffer technique but the test results were almost similar and therefore are not produced in this thesis.

5.2.2 Evaluation and Comments

From the test results, performance analysis and speedup curve, it is evident that the implementation of the buffer technique has improved the performance of the FDTD computation on GPU.

If noticed carefully it can be noted that for test 1 & 2, the buffer technique saves

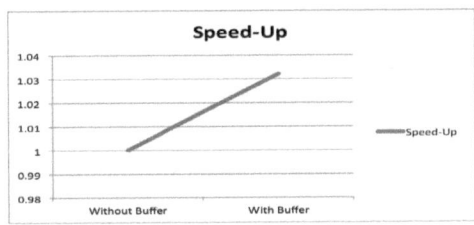

Figure 5.3: Speedup result of Test 3 & 4. *More is better*

1.2829 seconds at each time step because of buffer implementation. Therefore it can be deduced that the GPU spends 1.2829 seconds to access the memory (fetch & read) for data input/output at each time step in order to calculate the field variables of next time step. Whereas, for test 3 & 4, the buffer technique saves 0.4284 seconds at each time step because of buffer implementation. Therefore it can be deduced that the GPU spends 0.4284 seconds to access the memory (fetch & read) for data input/output at each time step in order to calculate the field variables of next time step.

It should also be noted that if the perofrmance at each time step for the tests on each input parameter conditions are taken into consideration then the amount of time spent for memory access by the GPU should be same, but the test results are proving otherwise. Therefore, it means that the time saved at each time-step is not just dependant on the memory accesses but on many other variables of computation as well. Another anomaly can be noticed while implementing the buffer technique on random excitation points (refer to Test 5 Result). For test 5, the produced results when compared to the results of test 2, shows that instead of improving the performance with buffer implementation for random points, the peformance of the program reduced. One possible explanation for this phenomenon can be that the GPU is storing the data input/output at random location and therefore, the memory access inside the GPU becomes uncoalesced in nature, thus, reducing the performance than it shpuld be. There can be many tests, which could verify this anomaly but because of time-constraint and limited time-period of the project, those tests could not be performed. This leaves a big space to improve the implementation even further to gain more efficient performance of data I/O of FDTD computation on GPU.

Chapter 6

Conclusion and Future Scope

In this Chapter, the effectiveness of the proposed solution is concluded and the future scopes and possibilities of improvement of the proposed method are discussed.

6.1 Future Scope

This thesis tries to provide solution to compensate the latency gap between main memory and the GPU, and optimize the memory access of GPU. Therefore, the solution proposed in this thesis can be implemented in any system that uses CUDA GPU computation. As reviewed from Chapter 1, CUDA has good potential of usage in near future and many heterogeneous parallel computing systems will use CUDA in order to improve the performance of softwares and parallel algorithms. Programs or softwares, starting from Game Industry to Scientific Computation, utilising the CUDA architecture and GPU computation can benefit from the solution methodlogy provided in this thesis. Again, the proposed solution, especially implementation of buffer for random excitation points in FDTD computation, is open to further improvements as reviewed in Chapter 5, therefore making room for even better performance gains.

6.2 Conclusion

As discussed in Chapter 1, because of the latency gap between the GPU and the main memory, it can be a bottleneck in performance. Since, FDTD computation requires to fetch the field values to compute the field values of next time step, therefore while computing FDTD on GPU, the GPU has to access the field values from the main memory quite often. Although FDTD computation on GPU are very efficient and perform very well, but the performance can be further enhanced if the data input/output (I/O) of FDTD computation is optimized to produce even better efficiency. In Chapter 2 and 3, different methods of computing FDTD on GPU using GPGPU techniques are discussed.

To solve the issue in hand, this thesis proposes and discusses the implementation of a novel solution of using programmatically designed data buffer, which is discussed in Chapter 4, to optimize the memory access of GPU in order to increase the efficiency of data I/O of FDTD computation on GPU. The speedup (performance) deduced from the results and analysis discussed in Chapter 5 proves that the implementation of buffer has been a success and the peformance of FDTD computation was improved.

Bibliography

[1] M. Wolfe et al. Cuda fortran programming guide and reference. *The Portland Group, Release*, 2012.

[2] Nvidia. Nvidia cuda c programming guide. *NVIDIA Corporation*, 120, 2011.

[3] K. Yee. Numerical solution of initial boundary value problems involving maxwell's equations in isotropic media. *Antennas and Propagation, IEEE Transactions*, May 1966.

[4] G. M. Amdahl. Validity of the single processor approach to achieving large scale computing capabilities. In *Proceedings of the ACM Spring Joint Computer Conference*. ACM, 1967.

[5] J. R. Gurd and G. D Riley. Study materials of comp60611: Parallel programs and their performance.

[6] J. Von Neumann. *The computer and the brain*. Yale University Press, 2012.

[7] J. L. Hennessy and D. A. Patterson. *Computer architecture: a quantitative approach*. Elsevier, 2012.

[8] C. Carvalho. The gap between processor and memory speeds. In *Proc. of IEEE International Conference on Control and Automation*, 2002.

[9] W. A Wulf and S. A. McKee. Hitting the memory wall: implications of the obvious. *ACM SIGARCH computer architecture news*, 23(1):20–24, 1995.

[10] L. Dagum and R. Menon. Openmp: an industry standard api for shared-memory programming. *Computational Science & Engineering, IEEE*, 5(1):46–55, 1998.

[11] W. Gropp, E. Lusk, and A. Skjellum. *Using MPI: portable parallel programming with the message-passing interface*, volume 1. MIT press, 1999.

[12] K. Fatahalian. From shader code to teraflop: How shader cores work. *Beyond Programmable Shading Course*, 2009.

[13] I. Buck, T. Foley, D. Horn, J. Sugerman, K. Fatahalian, M. Houston, and P. Hanrahan. Brook for gpus: stream computing on graphics hardware. In *ACM Transactions on Graphics (TOG)*, volume 23, pages 777–786. ACM, 2004.

[14] J. A. van Meel, A. Arnold, D. Frenkel, SF. Portegies Zwart, and R. G. Belleman. Harvesting graphics power for md simulations. *Molecular Simulation*, 34(3):259–266, 2008.

[15] E. Lindholm, J. Nickolls, S. Oberman, and J. Montrym. Nvidia tesla: A unified graphics and computing architecture. *IEEE Micro*, 28(2):39–55, 2008.

[16] R. Johnson. Gpu computing with cuda. Presentation at CScADS Workshop on Automatic Tuning, 2007, 2007.

[17] J. Nickolls. Gpu parallel computing architecture and cuda programming model. Presentation at Hot Chips 2007: NVIDIA GPU Parallel Computing Architecture, 2007, 2007.

[18] J. Sanders and E. Kandrot. *CUDA by example: an introduction to general-purpose GPU programming*. Addison-Wesley Professional, 2010.

[19] D. B. Kirk and W. H. Wen-mei. *Programming massively parallel processors: a hands-on approach*. Newnes, 2012.

[20] M. Harris. Unified memory in cuda 6, November 2013.

[21] F. Costen. *High Speed Computational Modeling in the Application of UWB Signals*. PhD thesis, University of Manchester, 2005.

[22] P. Debye. Polar molecules. Technical report, Dover, 1929.

[23] F. D. Hastings, J. B Schneider, and S. L. Broschat. A monte-carlo fdtd technique for rough surface scattering. *Antennas and Propagation, IEEE Transactions on*, 43(11):1183–1191, 1995.

[24] R. Scarmozzino, A. Gopinath, R. Pregla, and S. Helfert. Numerical techniques for modeling guided-wave photonic devices. *Selected Topics in Quantum Electronics, IEEE Journal of*, 6(1):150–162, 2000.

[25] S. Berntsen and S. N. Hornsleth. Retarded time absorbing boundary conditions. *Antennas and Propagation, IEEE Transactions on*, 42(8):1059–1064, 1994.

[26] P. G. Petropoulos. Reflectionless sponge layers as absorbing boundary conditions for the numerical solution of maxwell equations in rectangular, cylindrical, and spherical coordinates. *SIAM Journal on Applied Mathematics*, 60(3):1037–1058, 2000.

[27] A. H-D. Cheng and D. T. Cheng. Heritage and early history of the boundary element method. *Engineering Analysis with Boundary Elements*, 29(3):268–302, 2005.

[28] D. Givoli. Non-reflecting boundary conditions. *Journal of Computational Physics*, 94(1):1–29, 1991.

[29] G. Mur. Absorbing boundary conditions for the finite-difference approximation of the time-domain electromagnetic-field equations. *Electromagnetic Compatibility, IEEE Transactions on*, (4):377–382, 1981.

[30] R. L. Higdon. Absorbing boundary conditions for difference approximations to the multidimensional wave equation. *Mathematics of computation*, 47(176):437–459, 1986.

[31] B. Salski. *Application of semi-analytical algorithms in the finite-difference time-domain modeling of electromagnetic radiation and scattering problems*. PhD thesis, Ph. D. Thesis, Warsaw University of Technology, 2010.

[32] Nvidia. Approaches to gpu computing.

[33] J. Larkin. Fast gpu development with cuda libraries, 2012.

[34] Y. Yan, PGI, M. Wolfe, S. Chandrasekaran, and B. M. Chapman. Introduction to openacc directives.

[35] Y. Liu and Y. Xiao. Using gpu and openacc to accelerate the maze optimal routing algorithm. *Applied Mechanics and Materials*, 380:1338–1341, 2013.

[36] H. J. Eberl and R. Sudarsan. Openacc parallelisation for diffusion problems, applied to temperature distribution on a honeycomb around the bee brood: A worked example using bicgstab. In *Parallel Processing and Applied Mathematics*, pages 311–321. Springer, 2014.

[37] M. Livesey, J. F. Stack, F. Costen, T. Nanri, N. Nakashima, and S. Fujino. Development of a cuda implementation of the 3 d fdtd method. *IEEE Antennas & Propagation Magazine*, 54(5):186–195, 2012.

[38] T. Nagaoka and S. Watanabe. A gpu-based calculation using the three-dimensional fdtd method for electromagnetic field analysis. In *Engineering in Medicine and Biology Society (EMBC), 2010 Annual International Conference of the IEEE*, pages 327–330. IEEE, 2010.

[39] J. Chi, F. Liu, E. Weber, Y. Li, and S. Crozier. Gpu-accelerated fdtd modeling of radio-frequency field tissue interactions in high-field mri. *IEEE Transactions on Biomedical Engineering*, 58(6):1789–1796, June 2011.

[40] Z. Bo, X. Zheng-hui, R. Wu, L. Wei-ming, and S. Xin-qing. Accelerating fdtd algorithm using gpu computing. In *Proceedings of 2011 IEEE International Conference on Microwave Technology & Computational Electromagnetics (ICMTCE)*, pages 410–413. IEEE, 2011.

[41] M. Wolfe. Understanding the cuda data parallel threading model understanding the cuda data parallel threading mode, February 2010.

[42] Cornell University. Introduction to gpgpu and cuda programming: Memory coalescing.

[43] P. Micikevicius. M02: High performance computing with cuda: Optimizing cuda.

[44] R. A. Kirsch. Seac maintenance manual: The outscriber, 1953.

Appendix A

Survey Questions posted

A.1 Survey Questions posted via email and Research-gate OSN platform

Which parallelising technique (OpenMP/MPI/CUDA) would you prefer more?

*Required

Which industry do you belong to? *

Have you ever worked on parallel and multi-core computing projects before? *
○ Yes
○ No

Have you ever heard or worked on a project requiring CUDA programming for parallelisation in GPGPU before? *
○ Yes
○ No

Which programming technique would you prefer more for parallel and multicore computing?
○ OpenMP
○ MPI
○ CUDA Programming

Ratings for OpenMP *
How would you rate different features for OpenMP?

	1 (Weak)	2	3	4	5 (Strong)
Ease of Use	○	○	○	○	○
Performance achieved	○	○	○	○	○

Ratings for MPI *
How would you rate different features for MPI?

	1 (Weak)	2	3	4	5 (Strong)
Ease of Use	○	○	○	○	○
Performance achieved	○	○	○	○	○

Ratings for CUDA Programming *
How would you rate different features for CUDA Programming?

	1 (Weak)	2	3	4	5 (Strong)
Ease of Use	○	○	○	○	○
Performance achieved	○	○	○	○	○

Which one do you think will be more used in future (in coming 5 years)?
○ OpenMP
○ MPI
○ CUDA Programming (GPGPU parallelisation)

Submit

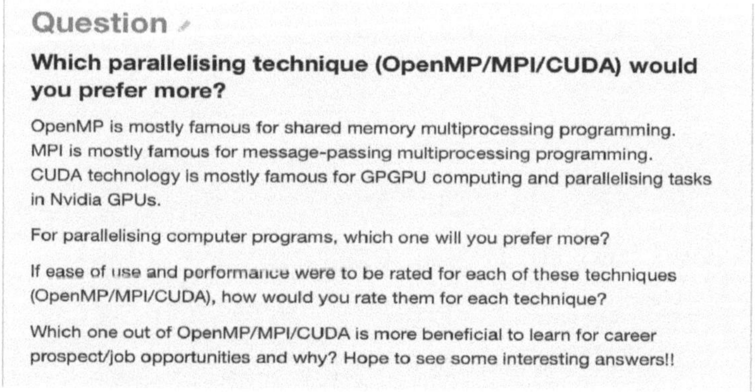

Question

Which parallelising technique (OpenMP/MPI/CUDA) would you prefer more?

OpenMP is mostly famous for shared memory multiprocessing programming. MPI is mostly famous for message-passing multiprocessing programming. CUDA technology is mostly famous for GPGPU computing and parallelising tasks in Nvidia GPUs.

For parallelising computer programs, which one will you prefer more?

If ease of use and performance were to be rated for each of these techniques (OpenMP/MPI/CUDA), how would you rate them for each technique?

Which one out of OpenMP/MPI/CUDA is more beneficial to learn for career prospect/job opportunities and why? Hope to see some interesting answers!!

Figure A.1: Question Posted via Researchgate OSN platform

SOMDIP DEY (born December 13, 1990 in Kolkata, India) is an Indian artificial intelligence scientist, technology journalist and serial entrepreneur. **He** is most notable for his work in making artificial intelligence affordable and accessible to developing countries. **Dey** currently works at the University of Essex and Samsung R&D Institute UK as an artificial intelligence researcher in embedded systems. One of his projects is "foodonomics". Foodonomics uses artificial intelligence and other computing technologies to reduce food waste. **Dey's** other research work includes developing algorithms in smartphones using artificial intelligence to learn the user's application usage behavior, and optimize the phone for improved performance, energy efficiency and the phone's temperature. **He** is also an editor of academic journals and magazines like Frontiers in Blockchain: Fourth Industrial Revolution and has previously served as an editor of ACM XRDS (Crossroads) magazine. He is also part of the technical program committee and reviewer of several top conferences such as IEEE CSCloud, IEEE EdgeCom, IEEE CSE, DAC, CVPR, ICCV.

YOUR KNOWLEDGE HAS VALUE

- We will publish your bachelor's and
  master's thesis, essays and papers

- Your own eBook and book -
  sold worldwide in all relevant shops

- Earn money with each sale

Upload your text at www.GRIN.com
and publish for free